MY BASQUE
CUISINE

MY BASQUE CUISINE

A Love Affair with Spanish Cooking

ASH MAIR

PHOTOGRAPHY BY JEAN CAZALS

Dedication

To Mum and my partner Begoña for their love and support towards everything I do.

Acknowledgements

I would like to thank the following people for their involvement in my life, career and help with this book.

First of all, thank you to my family for the continuous support I have received for everything I have strived to do throughout my career as a chef. Thanks for bringing me up in a creative environment and allowing me to believe in my dreams. Also, a special thanks to my brother Damien Mair and sister-in-law Robyn Kimber for their help with ideas on design and text for this book.

Professionally, I would like to thank each and every one of the chefs I have worked with since I first stepped into the kitchen—they have all, in one way or another, taught me so much. Thanks to my first teacher at culinary school, Paul Herbig, for teaching me discipline in the kitchen; John McCann for teaching me so much about classic techniques and French Cookery. And I would especially like to thank Rod Ascui and Kim Seagram for taking me under their wing and giving me so much support and inspiration from my beginnings as a young chef.

I would also like to say thank you to everyone who have helped me on this book. Jean Cazals for his fantastic photography. My beautiful partner Begoña for introducing me to the Basque country and her help with the translations throughout this book. Kontxi and Luken, my partner's parents, for all the great traditional Basque meals and hospitality I receive every time I visit the Basque country. Tony Licastro, Adam Mostowski and Michael Sanz from The Fishmongers Kitchen for their help with sourcing the fantastic seafood used in the development stages of this book.

I would also like to thank my agent Simon Romaniuk and the team from New Holland for bringing this all together and making my dream to write a book a possibility.

And finally, a special thanks to Karen Ross, Lucy Hards, Jimmy Foggo and the rest of the crew from Shine TV for my time on Professional MasterChef UK. And last but not least, Monica Galetti, Gregg Wallace and Michel Roux Jr for their belief in me through my MasterChef journey and their on-going support.

This edition published in 2016 by New Holland Publishers Pty Ltd
London • Sydney • Auckland

The Chandlery, Unit 704, 50 Westminster Bridge Road, London SE1 7QY, United Kingdom.
1/66 Gibbes Street, Chatswood, NSW 2067, Australia.
5/39 Woodside Ave, Northcote, Auckland 0627, New Zealand.

www.newhollandpublishers.com

ISBN 9781742578644

Managing Director: Fiona Schultz
Publisher: Alan Whiticker
Project Editor: Jessica McNamara
Cover design: Tracy Loughlin and Lorena Susak
Designer: Tracy Loughlin
Production Director: Olga Dementiev
Printer: Times Offset Malaysia

10 9 8 7 6 5 4 3 2 1

Keep up with New Holland Publishers on Facebook
www.facebook.com/NewHollandPublishers

CONTENTS

Foreword

The first time I heard about Ash was through a text message from Monica Galetti, my trusty Kiwi sous chef and co-host from *MasterChef: The Professionals*.

The text was short to the point and with a touch of wry humour. It read: "I think we have a winner, shame he's a bloody Aussie!" Up until then most of her daily texts to fill me in on how the skills tests were progressing were not very positive.

My first taste of food that Ash cooked for myself and Gregg at the MasterChef kitchen was hake with clams and ham. The dish was a triumph; delicate, beautiful, perfectly cooked and it had a trueness that was palpable to all the senses. Throughout the fierce competition Ash impressed with his knowledge and passion for all that is Basque. Robust in its origins, this cuisine in the hands of a master is not just exquisite but a revelation.

By the time we got to the final week the stress of the competition was starting to tell on Ash and at times he was doubled over with pain brought on from his anguish, nerves and lack of sleep. Ash won the title and our hearts with his desire, skills and indefatigable quest for Basque cuisine. I am thankful to have got to know Ash and he is what I would call a chef's chef. And of course Monica was right…he is a winner.

Michel Roux Jr

My cooking

Nere sukaldea

Mi cocina

IT WAS LATE SUMMER 2000 WHEN I MADE MY FIRST VISIT TO SPAIN, little realising how much it would influence my life and, more importantly, my career as a chef. I had spent the last couple of years travelling between my home of Tasmania and London, working the alternating summers, and had always been particularly keen to visit France and Spain to further my culinary knowledge.

My third summer working in London was coming to an end when I received a phone call from a mate asking me if I wanted a cheap flight out of London the following week for a bit of a break. Back then I was pretty happy not to do much planning so I said, "Sure, where to?" Twenty minutes later he called back and informed me that we were booked to fly to Barcelona.

I was finally on my way to one of my top culinary destinations that I had read so much about during my first years as a chef. I already knew about the food culture in Spain including the traditions of the family meals as well as the ground-breaking restaurants such as Ferran Adria's El Bulli and now I would get a taste of it. I spent my first few days in Barcelona blown away by the vibrancy of the city, the culture
and most importantly the food. We made a point of avoiding anywhere that had menus in English. I don't know how we got around, with zero Spanish and no English-speakers in many of the hidden little bars and restaurants we found ourselves in. It was all the more exciting not knowing what we were ordering and made for some interesting meals.

I remember my first *menú del día* clearly. First off we had *judías verdes con jamón* (runner beans simply cooked with chunks of serrano ham). We followed this with *meluza a la plancha con patatas panaderas* (grilled hake with potatoes cooked with onions) then by the classic dessert *crema catalana*. I reflected on how good that meal was. It was simple but it tasted so good.

Wandering around the streets of Barcelona I was struck by the quality of the produce that was readily available throughout the city. The fresh seafood, fruit and vegetables bursting with colour and flavour set against a backdrop of chorizos, jamones and preserved vegetables. I'd found food heaven and I was hooked. I've continued to visit Spain for inspiration, to enjoy its culture and most importantly to eat. I discovered something new every time. The food I have enjoyed has been amazingly fresh, vibrant and full of comforting, robust flavours that make me want to dive in for more.

Returning home after each trip full of new ideas and influences, I set out to create or re-create the dishes and flavours that influenced me during my time away. *Basque Cuisine* contains a collection of these recipes. In essence many of these aren't 'mine', having been passed to me by chefs, friends or extended family in Spain. The rest have been created from something I have seen or tasted. Each has been written with the home kitchen in mind. To make Spanish cooking accessible, I have refrained from using difficult-to-find ingredients for some of the more traditional dishes, substituting easier-to-source alternatives that taste every bit as good.

Most of the recipes are relatively simple to prepare, without any specialist equipment. Some, particularly the sweet dishes, do require a more technical approach, but don't let this put you off. Save these for the weekend or when you're not too pressed for time. Most of all, enjoy the wonderful food of Spain.

The food of Spain and the Basque Country

Espainia eta Euskal Herriko gastronomia

La gastronomía de España y País Vasco

TO SAY THE SPANISH ENJOY THEIR FOOD IS AN UNDERSTATEMENT. The people of the Basque region take cooking to another level in which gastronomy is a way of life. For the Spanish, good food is a necessity and it's true to say that much of the nation's day-to-day living revolves around it. The Spanish still make time to cook and eat together and it's an important part of socialising with family and friends.

Traditionally lunch, or *almuerzo,* is the most important meal of the day and often contains multiple courses or dishes while dinner, or *cena,* is usually a smaller meal often eaten quite late at night by European standards. This may or may not have something to do with the common practice of enjoying tapas and pintxos in the afternoon or on the way home after work.

Through geographical differences and proximity to the ocean, each of Spain's regions have many unique dishes of their own and these are often borrowed and modified by neighbouring regions utilising ingredients local to the area. For instance, a tortilla prepared in the northern regions of Spain will commonly contain salt cod and green peppers while in the south it might contain a mixture of offal, but essentially it is the same dish.

Throughout Spain's history the cuisine has been influenced by many events most notably the invasion by the Romans in BC218, then the Moorish conquest in 711AD as well as Spain's exploration of the new world. Each brought new ingredients such as lentils, spices, potatoes and tomatoes, now all important ingredients in Spanish cuisine. New techniques and methods of preservation were also introduced such as *escabeche,* in which fish and meats are preserved in acidic, vinegar-based sauces. At the same time, the Basque people were creating a cuisine of their own, rich in seafood from the Cantabrian Sea, as well as meat and dairy from the fertile mountain ranges. The Basque Country enjoys high rainfall making it perfect for the cultivation of a large range of fruit, nuts and vegetables.

There are many similarities of the cuisine throughout all the regions of Spain, but the food of the Basque Country seems to stand out the most. With around 14 per cent of the Basque Country actually within the borders of France, many French influences are obvious in Basque recipes.

To this day the Basques are very proud of their cuisine and it seems they've been more than happy to keep it to themselves. The word is spreading though, and cities such as San Sebastian and Bilbao are now considered some of the world's great gastronomical destinations.

Many of Spain's classic dishes are actually the product of poverty, stemming from a time when the population had nothing but cheap and quite humble ingredients available, such as eggs, pulses and garlic. The dish *migas* is a prime example in which stale bread is fried with any other available ingredients, transforming it into a rustic but fulfilling and beautiful dish.

Unlike modern Spanish cooking conjured up by chefs such as Ferran Adrià and Andoni Aduriz, the traditional food of Spain and the Basque Country is a simple affair, making it perfect for the home cook. Like other Mediterranean countries, the food is very healthy, containing lots of fresh vegetables, seafood, pulses and olive oil. Spanish food is about sharing and that's also how I like to present my food. I recommend preparing four different tapas for a light meal. The rest of the dishes serve four as part of a meal, which I recommend is made up of at least two courses, such as a soup and a main course, or a main dish and a dessert, or a full three or even four-course meal, if you prefer. Sides and vegetable dishes are also a great addition to a meal, or can be enjoyed simply on their own.

Some recipes need quite specific measurements especially the sweet ones, so I suggest buying a good set of scales and some measuring spoons. Most of the other recipes are quite forgiving and measurements don't have to be as specific. Cooking needn't be a rigid process, so feel free to add or take away ingredients as you please. Sometimes things work and sometimes they don't. That's actually one of the great things about cooking – it can be unpredictable, sometimes surprising and always fulfilling. In the world of food every day is different and it's always exciting. That's why I love to cook. How about you?

PANTRY

Jakitokia

DESPENSA

MOST KITCHENS THROUGHOUT SPAIN and the Basque Country have a small pantry of essential dry and preserved goods, with most households preferring to shop for fresh ingredients on a daily basis. The daily shopping is an important part of the community culture, where any chance for a bit of socialising is a good one. It's also a guarantee of cooking with the freshest and best quality produce, which is of utmost importance to good cooking.

Most of the ingredients in this book are easy to find though I do recommend finding a good Spanish delicatessen for chorizos, jamón and other cured Spanish meats. Most will also have a good range of olive oil to cook with, as well as good Spanish wines to enjoy with your meal.

Whatever ingredients you buy, make sure they are the best quality you can afford. Look for good small independent green grocers, butchers and fishmongers where you will not only find great produce, but more often than not you will get good advice on what to do with it.

ALMONDS (ALMENDRAS)

Spain is the world's second largest producer of almonds after the USA and they are utilised in every aspect of Spanish cooking from snacks to sauces, soups and desserts. All of the recipes in this book use either blanched (skinless) almonds or flaked. Store almonds in an airtight container away from any foodstuffs with a strong odour as they tend to absorb other flavours, which can taint the dishes they are used in.

BEEF (CARNE DE VACA/BUEY)

Scattered across the jagged hills of the Basque Country, traditional cider houses or *sagardotegi* serve some of the most amazing beef I've tasted. The grass-fed cattle are slaughtered quite old, at around 5 years. The favourite cut in Spain is thick slabs of forerib called *txuletón*, which are grilled over coals, creating a charred smoky crust and rare inside, served with nothing more than a sprinkling of good sea salt.

The most flavourful cuts of beef are from the muscles that do the most work such as the cheeks and shins, but they are also the toughest and benefit from long, slow cooking. It's worth taking the time to cook these cuts, as a lovely slow braise or cocido of shin or cheek is the definition of comfort food. The amazing depth of flavour and melt in your mouth texture is hard to beat. These cuts are also much cheaper than prime cuts of beef, though sirloin and fillet are also great, benefiting from quick cooking on a hot grill.

CORN MAIZE

Not to be confused with polents, corn maize is a type of coarsely ground cornflour available in Spanish and Latin delicatessens. It is similar to Italian polenta but is more finely ground. Two varieties are available, *harina de maiz blanco* (white) and *harina de maiz amarillo* (yellow).

EGGS (HUEVOS)

I always use fresh, free-range organic eggs for cooking, which are ethically produced and have a superior flavour. The recipes in this book use medium-sized eggs weighing around 65 g (2½ oz) each. In Spain eggs are commonly eaten for lunch or in the evening in dishes such as *tortilla de patatas* (potato omelette) or *revuelto de hongos* or *revuelto de gambas* (eggs scrambled with mushrooms or prawns).

FISH AND SHELLFISH (PESCADOS Y MARISCOS)

When cooking fish and shellfish it's of the utmost importance that the seafood is as fresh as possible. Seafood is an essential part of the Spanish diet and it's common for Spanish families to eat some every day.

When choosing fish and shellfish the smell is always a good sign of freshness. Fresh seafood should smell of the sea and not have a strong fishy scent at all. The flesh of any fish should feel firm to the touch and it should have bright clear eyes with clean looking, bright red gills.

Molluscs like mussels and clams should feel heavy for their weight and the shells should be closed or only slightly open. Give them a bit of a shake and any open shells should slowly close, if not they may be dead so discard them. Any mussels that don't open after cooking are probably bad so avoid eating them. Shellfish such as prawns, langoustines and lobster should also feel heavy for their weight; have bright shiny shells and smell of the sea.

Purging Clams and Cockles

Clams and cockles should be purged before cooking to remove any sand and grit. Many fishmongers sell clams and cockles already purged so ask when buying, though you can easily do it yourself at home:

Whisk 30 g (1 oz) of fine sea salt into 1 litre (1¾ pints) of cold water until dissolved. Place the clams or cockles in a bowl, pour over the salt solution then sprinkle over a handful of rolled oats or flour. Refrigerate for at least 5 hours and the grit will be expelled from the shells. Drain and rinse in cold water before cooking.

Salt Cod (Bacalao)

Bacalao, or salt cod, is simply cod that has been heavily salted and dried as a method of preservation. The process also affects the texture and enhances the flavour. Traditionally dried on wooden racks or hanging from stone cliffs bacalao is now commonly prepared in commercial drying rooms.

Salt cod is readily available from Spanish and Caribbean suppliers. You can make your own version at home. Due to the drying method it won't be exactly the same as a purchased product but still perfectly acceptable for the recipes in this book.

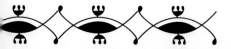

FIDEOS

In Spain any type of noodle is referred to as *fideos*, but this term most commonly describes the short noodles used to cook the Catalan dish of *Fideua*. Fideua is very similar to classic paella but the rice is replaced with fideo noodles. The noodles are generally short ranging from 2 to 5 cm (¾ to 2 in) long and come in a range of thicknesses. If you can't find fideo noodles you can make a good substitute with thin spaghetti. Wrap it in a kitchen towel and run it over the edge of a table while pulling down to snap the spaghetti into short pieces.

GARLIC (AJO)

Garlic is significant to many of the dishes in this book. Throughout Spain it would be hard to find any household that didn't have a good supply of garlic to hand. The Spanish consume a huge amount – around 4 kg (8 lb) per head every year. When choosing garlic buy whole heads and check their quality by their weight, the heavier the better. Avoid pre-prepared garlic of any kind as it just doesn't deliver the same flavour as freshly prepared garlic. Many recipes in this book call for fresh sliced garlic, which is important to the overall flavour of the dish.

HERBS (HIERBAS)

The use of herbs in traditional Spanish cooking is kept to a minimum, with most additional flavourings coming from dried spices. The most popular herb is parsley (*perejil*), commonly used in sauces for dishes such as *merluza en salsa verde* (hake in green sauce) or for garnishing. Store any fresh herbs refrigerated in their original packaging or wrap them in a damp (not wet) sheet of absorbent kitchen paper.

Bay leaves are a common flavouring in sauces, braises and stews. Personally, I prefer dried bay leaves over fresh, since fresh can add an unpleasant bitterness to dishes. Dried bay leaves have a mellower, more rounded flavour. Remove them from any dish you use them in before serving.

LAMB (CORDERO)

The Spanish like to eat lamb when it's young and extremely tender. *Lechazo* (milk fed lamb) is popular, especially in central Spain where young animals, barely one month old, are roasted whole and served with simple side dishes such as *patatas panadera* (potatoes cooked with

onion and peppers). All through the Pyrenees, *cordero al chilindrón* (slow-cooked lamb stew) is a popular dish of lamb slowly stewed, which makes good use of older beasts, and is a perfect preparation for cheaper cuts such as shanks, shoulder and neck.

Like beef, the cheaper cuts of lamb can also be the tastiest when treated properly. One of my favourites, lamb neck, is great simply braised on the bone until the meat is as tender as butter, then served with some puréed potato.

LEGUMES (LEGUMBRES)

A cheaper alternative to meat, which was a luxury to the poor throughout Spain, dried legumes also provide nutrients and fibre through the winter. Legumes continue to be extremely popular today with speciality shops selling different types of these tasty little morsels in fresh, dried or preserved form. Quite often these shops have a queue of people out the door and down the street at busy times.

Most legumes need soaking before cooking so a little planning is required when cooking your own, or substitute with pre-cooked canned varieties.

Beans (Alubias)

Spain produces some fantastic beans and there are a number of towns known specifically for their bean and bean dishes. The town of Tolosa in the Basque region of northern Spain holds an annual four-day festival to celebrate the local *Alubia de Tolosa*, the small black bean the town is known for. Cooked in a simple vegetable broth then traditionally served with cabbage, *morcilla* and Guindilla peppers, *Alubias de Tolosa* are truly outstanding. However, as they are difficult to find outside Spain these particular beans are not included here.

However, I have included a recipe for *Fabada*, a rich bean stew from Asturias, which is made with *Fabes la granja*, which can be successfully substituted with butter or cannellini beans. Fabada is perhaps Spain's most popular bean dish, and just about every supermarket sells a canned version, making it as popular in Spain as baked beans is in the United Kingdom.

When buying beans, even dried beans, make sure to buy them as fresh as possible. As dried beans get older they take longer to cook and the shells become tougher. When cooking beans, make sure to soak them for a full 24 hours, if possible. Remember not to season the water they are cooked in until the beans are just about ready, or it will make the shells tough.

As with other legumes, you can substitute canned beans, drained and rinsed thoroughly, in most recipes.

CHICKPEAS (GARBANZOS)

Chickpeas or garbanzo beans were introduced into Spain by the Moors. They are now a common ingredient in soups and braises across the country.

Dried chickpeas do require a long soak in cold water before cooking but if you're short of time use canned chickpeas instead. Just makes sure to rinse off the brine before using.

LENTILS (LENTEJAS)

One of the first crops domesticated by humans, lentils are an important food source throughout the world. Packed with protein and amino acids they are also considered to be one of the world's healthiest foods.

Thought to have been introduced to Spain by Roman soldiers for whom lentils were part of daily rations, they are now a popular legume used in various soups and stews. The most common lentils eaten in Spain are the small green or brown type. Unlike many other legumes lentils need no soaking before cooking, which makes them the perfect healthy fast food.

MUSHROOMS (SETAS)

This is a popular ingredient, mainly in the northern regions of Spain where foraging for wild produce is extremely popular. There are even mushroom-foraging tours and cooking classes to show cooks how to prepare their bounty. In some areas the popularity of the tours is such that local governments have introduced an annual fee for amateur foragers and a daily limit on takings. Ceps, chanterelles and saffron milk cap are quite common and the odd truffle can be found also.

When purchasing mushrooms avoid anything that looks wet or slimy. Store mushrooms refrigerated in a loosely closed paper bag. Avoid washing mushrooms if you can, simply brush off any dirt with a soft brush. If you must wash them, dunk them into a sink of cold water and swish around with your hand for about 10 seconds then remove from the water and drain. Immediately pat the mushrooms dry with kitchen paper to stop them absorbing too much water. Washed mushrooms go slimy very quickly if stored, so cook them straightaway.

OLIVE OIL (ACEITE DE OLIVA)

Spain is the world's largest producer of olive oil, manufacturing around 45 per cent of its annual production. Consumption is also high; the annual rate is nearly 15 litres (26 pints) per person.

It's a good idea to have a few different olive oils in you cupboard at home. Most important is a good extra virgin oil, as well as a mild or 'blended' oil. Avoid using virgin olive oil for cooking and save it for dressings and for drizzling over bread, salads or finished dishes. For cooking, use a light olive oil blend, or even vegetable or sunflower oil, especially for sautéing.

Two main methods are used to extract the oil from the fruit; mechanical and chemical. The mechanical method simply 'presses' the oil from the fruit and is used to create virgin and extra virgin oil. Extra virgin oil has the best flavour and the least acid content. The acid percentage of the oil is an indicator of its quality, the less acid the content the better quality the oil is deemed to be. After the initial pressing of the fruit the pulverised flesh and stones are called pomace. Pomace is treated chemically and sometimes with heat to extract the remaining oil to produce 'pomace' oil. This is refined and blended with virgin olive oil to be sold as 'olive pomace oil'.

Refined olive oils are simply low quality virgin oils that have been filtered to remove unpleasant flavours and excess acid. These are usually sold labelled simply as 'olive oil' or 'light olive oil'.

Store olive oil in a cool, dark place. Light and fluctuations in temperature can damage the oil and make it go rancid.

OLIVES (ACEITUNAS)

Spain's olive production is staggeringly high with approximately 300 million olive trees producing more than 6 million tons of fruit per year. Most are processed into olive oil but a huge amount are cured, marinated and also stuffed for eating.

Spain produces more than 250 types of eating olives but probably the most popular is the *manzanilla* or 'little apple', which is commonly available outside of Spain. Green olives like the manzanilla are picked before they are fully ripe, which gives them a stronger and more bitter flavour than their fully ripened black olives.

A few varieties of olives can be eaten fresh, but the majority need to be treated usually by wet or dry brining to remove the unpalatable bitter compounds. The olives can then be marinated in oil, kept in brine or stuffed with a filling such as almond, red pepper or anchovy, all of which are

popular. Olives are the perfect accompaniment to drinks or to the start of a meal, and as such every bar, restaurant and home across Spain will offer olives as a welcoming snack to their guests.

ONIONS (CEBOLLA)

All the recipes in this book use the common Spanish (Bermuda) brown onion, unless specified otherwise. If you want to be really particular, for the recipes in this book, a small onion weighs about 100 g (3½ oz); medium about 150 g (5¼ oz); and large about 200 g (7 oz).

Store onions in a cool dark cupboard and discard them if they start to shoot. Onions really don't need to be stored in the refrigerator but I do find that chilled onions seem to be less of an eye irritant when cutting. For any dish that contains raw onion soak the peeled and chopped onion in cold water for 10 minutes then pat dry with a paper towel to remove the harsh onion flavour while preserving its natural sweetness.

PAPRIKA (PIMENTÓN)

Paprika is produced by drying various types of capsicums and/or chilli peppers and is available in two main varieties, *dulce* (sweet) and *picante* (hot). In Spain another common version, *ahumado* (smoked paprika), is produced by smoke-drying the peppers over oak. Smoked paprika also comes in mild, medium and hot versions and all add a wonderful smokiness to whatever they are added to.

Commonly you will see smoked paprika labelled *Pimentón De La Vera* which is only produced in Vera, Extremadura. It's protected by its own D.O. (Denominations of Origin) and is considered the best smoked paprika available.

PORK (CERDO)

Anyone who has visited Spain will know just how much the Spanish love pork. Walk into any supermarket or delicatessen and it's hard to miss the walls of, jamón, chorizos and salchichón adorning counters, almost hiding everything else behind them. Along with all the cured pork products, fresh pork is also commonly consumed throughout the country. It's still quite common for families in rural areas to rear and slaughter their own pigs. The better cuts are usually eaten fresh while the cheaper cuts are turned into cured jamón, sausages and blood puddings.

Lesser cuts have become more popular and can be found in supermarkets and butchers. Belly, cheeks, shoulder and ribs are all worth searching out and preparing.

I only buy free-range or organic pork for its superior flavour and to support an ethical farming practice.

Blood Sausage (Morcilla)

Morcilla, the Spanish version of blood pudding, is made with pigs' blood, pigs' fat and different spices, depending on the region of production. Spanish morcilla generally comes in two types *morcilla de arroz*, which is studded with cooked rice and *morcilla de cebolla,* which contains a high proportion of onion. I prefer the former which, when fried, develops a fantastic crispy crust and is most enjoyable served simply with poached eggs. There are also fully cured versions of morcilla, which can be thinly sliced and consumed without cooking, however, they can be difficult to find outside Spain. Spanish delicatessens will sell at least one variety of morcilla, and they are interchangeable in any recipe. If you can't find morcilla, a good black pudding will substitute.

Chorizo

A pork-based dry-cured sausage, chorizo comes in as many varieties as Spain has villages. Chorizo generally comes in *dulce* (sweet) and *picante* (hot) varieties usually spiced with sweet or hot, smoked or un-smoked paprika, as well as garlic and other spices. Chorizo has become incredibly popular in recent years, finding its way into many fine dining kitchens throughout the world.

The fully cured varieties can be eaten thinly sliced as a tapa or on bread, but the fresher, partially cured varieties need to be cooked before eating. Cooking chorizo releases lovely red paprika-flavoured oil that enriches anything it is cooked with, but take care as it can easily overpower other flavours and make dishes too oily. For the health conscious, chorizo can be simmered in water for 5 minutes to extract some of the fat before adding to a dish.

Spanish Ham (Jamón)

Jamón has become increasingly popular in the last few years and is now widely available outside of Spain, with many leading supermarkets selling a quality product.

Jamón is prepared by trimming and packing pork legs in salt, allowing one day for each 1 kg (2 lb) of meat, to draw out excess moisture. The salt is then washed off and the legs are hung and left to air-dry before being moved to a controlled environment to cure for anything up to 3 years before being ready for sale.

Spanish jamón is produced in various grades of quality and price depending on the breed of pig and its feed. *Jamón ibérico*, the best and most expensive jamón, come from the black Iberian pig and are produced in three main grades:

Jamón ibérico de bellota, the finest, is produced from black Iberian pigs that feed entirely on acorns, giving the ham a distinctive flavour. It is cured for at least 30 months.

Jamón ibérico de recebo is fed on a mixture of acorns and grain and has a shorter curing time of around 24 months. *Jamón ibérico de cebo*, commonly called *Jamón ibérico*, is solely grain fed and is also cured for up to 24 months.

By far the most common Spanish ham, *jamón serrano* is produced in the same way but from a more common breed or white pig, and is generally grain-fed only. The curing time is also shorter but it lacks the depth of flavour of the more superior acorn-fed varieties. Jamón serrano makes up around 90 per cent of Spain's annual production of hams and is relatively cheap compared to the ibérico varieties, and is commonly available outside of Spain.

For cooking I suggest using jamón serrano simply because of the price difference and save the jamón ibérico for enjoying with a glass of sherry.

POTATOES (PATATAS)

Spanish conquistadors first encountered the potato in Peru in the early 1500s where the native Incas had been eating them for hundreds of years. Slowly they found their way on to the Spanish galleons as basic rations before being taken to Spain, from where they were introduced to the rest of Europe.

There are early records of potatoes being consumed in households in Spain but people in Europe were sceptical thinking potatoes were unfit for human consumption. As the potato spread throughout Europe, usually grown for animal feed, governments discovered its importance as staple foodstuff and started promoting its cultivation and consumption.

Hundreds of varieties of potatoes are now available commercially and the main thing is to select a type with characteristics that are appropriate for the recipe it will be used in. Most potatoes fall within two groups: starchy or waxy. Starchy potatoes will soften and fall apart when cooked so are great for mash, baking and frying. Waxier varieties will hold their shape better when cooked and are less prone to falling apart in salads and soups.

POULTRY (AVES)

CHICKEN (POLLO)

I choose flavourful free-range and corn-fed varieties of poultry. Always buy chicken on the bone, if possible, and before, or even after cooking, freeze the bones until you have enough to make your own stock. Like other meats, the cheaper cuts of chicken such as the legs and thighs are the most flavourful compared to the more expensive breast meat.

Many people remove the skin for health reasons. I recommend doing this after cooking since it helps keep the flesh moist while cooking and also adds flavour.

Spain has many popular chicken dishes including *pollo al ajillo* (chicken cooked with garlic), which is served in bars and restaurants all over the country.

QUAIL (CODORNICES)

Looking like miniature chicken, quail are fiddly to prepare, but have a great, mildly gamey flavour making them an interesting alternative to chicken. Farm-raised quail is available all year round.

Quail can be cooked in different ways, too. In Spain, it's not uncommon to find quail marinated in *escabeche*, an acidic, sauce-like vinaigrette, which was originally used as a form of preservation. They can be roasted whole or flattened and grilled over coals or even confit in duck fat. As with chicken, look for free-range birds, which will have lived a happier life and be superior in flavour.

PIQUILLO PEPPERS (PIMIENTOS DE PIQUILLO)

Protected by a DOP, *pimientos de piquillo* are cultivated in and around the village of Lodosa in the Navarre region of Spain. After picking, the bright red peppers are roasted over smoking embers, which gives them a subtle yet rich smoky flavour, before being seeded and packed in

jars or cans. Commonly served in pintxo bars across the north of Spain, their small size and shape make them perfect little sacks for stuffing, to make dishes such as *pimientos rellenos de bacalao* (peppers stuffed with salt cod)

RICE (ARROZ)

Rice is another ingredient introduced to Spain by the Moors, and quickly became an important staple used in many traditional dishes, especially paella, which is probably the most well-known Spanish dish of all. Andalucía is Spain's primary rice-producing region, but the best rice is said to be *Arroz bomba* and *Arroz Calasparra*, cultivated in Valencia and Murcia respectively. Calasparra was awarded its own DOP in 1986, and is only produced in small quantities in the region in the province of Murcia.

The *Bomba* plant is rather unproductive and takes a long time to mature, which in turn makes it quite expensive compared to other varieties. The short plump grain has the ability to absorb more liquid than other strains making it very flavourful. Interestingly it only expands widthways when cooked. Using the right rice to make paella is important to achieve results so I suggest that if you don't have a suitable paella rice then cook something else instead.

SALT (SAL)

Salt is important to the taste of food and it is one of the simple reasons that food in restaurants often surpasses the flavour of food at home. Chefs taste and season as they cook enhancing the flavours of the ingredients. This doesn't mean food has to be salty though, just add a few grains and you'll notice a difference to everything you cook. It's easy to add a little more if needed, but if you add too much there's no way to remove the flavour.

Use a natural flaked sea salt in all your cooking and avoid any fine 'table salts'. The latter may be cheaper but often contains anti-caking agents so you'll need to add more to achieve the same results in seasoning, which makes it less healthy.

SHERRY (JEREZ)

Sherry, a fortified wine produced near the town of Jerez, has seen a resurgence in popularity in recent years after being considered a cheap cooking wine for so many years outside of Spain.

Fermented from white grapes then fortified and aged in a series of oak barrels before being bottled, sherry is produced in a number of different varieties, from dry to sweet.

Much loved as an aperitif throughout Spain, sherry is also a common ingredient used in cooking many traditional dishes. The most common sherries used in cooking are *Fino* or *Manzanilla* but a sweetened Oloroso (*Oloroso Amoroso*) sherry is also good for cooking anything that benefits from a touch of sweetness. Sherries made from Pedro Ximenez, or moscatel grapes, which are very sweet, are great for using in dessert dishes.

BASICS

Oinarriak

BÁSICOS

MANY OF THE DISHES IN THIS BOOK RELY ON SIMPLE PREPARATIONS and most are easy to prepare.

There is really no substitute for a good, homemade stock but some supermarkets now sell quality fresh stocks, which are more than adequate for the dishes in this book. However, if you can, it's always better to make your own at home and you'll be rewarded with a true depth of flavour in the final dish and have greater fulfilment in what you have created.

Wherever possible, avoid using stock cubes and concentrates, as these are often over salty and insipid, resulting in flat-tasting food with watery sauces.

Freshly made stocks will keep well in the refrigerator for a few days and can be frozen to use later, so make a decent-sized batch so you always have good quality stock to hand.

Garlic and parsley oil
Baratxuri eta perrexil olioa
Aceite de ajo y perejil

The perfect flavour enhancer, *aceite de ajo y perejil* is so useful in the kitchen it's always worth having a supply. Used extensively in Spanish cooking, it's usually added during or near the end of cooking to stop the garlic from burning, which can add an unpleasant bitter flavour.

At home it's great for adding flavour to just about anything. Add a small spoonful to sautéed mushrooms near the end of cooking or pour over fish or meat as it cooks to boost the flavour. Aceite de ajo y perejil also works perfectly as a marinade for all types of meat and fish – but use it sparingly, unless you really love garlic!

MAKES ABOUT 120 ML (4½ FL OZ)
100 ml (3½ fl oz) olive oil
5 garlic cloves, peeled and finely chopped
3 tablespoons finely chopped flat leaf parsley

Simply mix the olive oil, garlic and parsley together. *Aceite de ajo y perejil* keeps well in the fridge for up to a week.

Bread crisps
Ogi kurruskaria
Pan crujiente

Easy to make and also a good way to use up any stale bread, a bowl of *pan crujiente* is perfect to serve with dips or as a base for canapés and pintxos. You can use white or brown baguette or for a really light, crisp texture use a good ciabatta or focaccia. Pan crujiente will keep well for a couple of days in an airtight container.

MAKE 35–40 CRISPS
Olive oil for drizzling
1 small baguette or ciabatta about 30 cm (12 in) long
Coarse sea salt

Preheat the oven to 275°F/140°C/Gas mark 1.

Drizzle olive oil over a baking tray to make a thin film.

Slice the baguette on an angle into 5 mm (¼ in) slices and rub both sides of the bread on the tray so each side has a thin coat of oil. Add more oil to the tray as required, but don't soak the bread slices.

Spread the slices in a single layer on the baking tray and sprinkle with a little coarse sea salt. Bake for 10–15 minutes or until slightly golden and crisp. Leave to cool completely before serving. Store in an airtight container.

Fish stock
Arrain-salda
Caldo de pescado

A good fish stock is an important base to many of the dishes featured in *My Basque Cuisine*. Making your own is really easy and also one of the fastest stocks to make. Bones from a firm white fish such as cod or turbot are best. Bones from oily fish can make the stock turn cloudy.

MAKES ABOUT 2 LITRES (3½ PINTS)
2 kg (4½ lb) white fish bones, including heads
4 celery sticks, roughly chopped
2 large onions, peeled and roughly chopped
½ leek, white part only, rinsed and roughly chopped
3 garlic cloves, peeled
1 bay leaf
small handful parsley stalks
2 sprigs thyme
2.5 litres (4 ½ pints) water

Rinse the fish bones under cold running water, then place them in a stock pot with all the vegetables and herbs. Cover with the water, then bring to a simmer. Skim off any scum that rises to the surface and continue simmering for 30 minutes.

Remove from the heat and leave to rest for 15 minutes then pass through a fine sieve, reserving the liquid and discarding the bones and vegetables. Leave to go cold. Refrigerate and use within 3 days or freeze for up to 3 months.

Brown chicken stock
Oilasko-salda iluna
Caldo oscuro de pollo

Use this stock in braises and for making last-minute sauces and gravy. As with other stocks remember to skim any impurities that rise to the surface during cooking. Pass it through a couple of layers of muslin (cheese cloth) to remove any small particles before using.

MAKES 2 LITRES (3½ PINTS)
2 kg (4½ lb) chicken wings (or any other chicken bones you may have saved)
2.5 litres (4½ pints) water
2 medium carrots, peeled and roughly chopped
2 large onions, peeled and roughly chopped
1 medium leek, white part only, rinsed and roughly chopped
2 garlic cloves, peeled
1 bay leaf
2 sprigs of thyme

Preheat the oven to 375°F/190°C/Gas mark 5. Place the chicken wings in a deep roasting tray and roast for 15 minutes or until golden. Turn the wings and cook for another 15 minutes or until deep brown. Remove from the oven and tip into a colander to drain off the fat.

Place the carrot, onion and leek in the same tray and roast for 20 minutes or until lightly golden.

Put the chicken wings in a stock pot and cover with the water. Bring to the boil over a high heat, then reduce to a simmer, skimming the surface of any scum as it rises.

Add the roast vegetables, garlic and herbs, then bring back to a simmer.

Continue to simmer gently for 4½ hours, skimming scum from the surface every 30 minutes.

Remove from the heat and leave to rest for 15 minutes before passing the stock through a fine sieve into a bowl. Discard the chicken, bones and vegetables. Leave to go cold then refrigerate the liquid, or use straightaway. Once refrigerated the stock will be quite gelatinous and develop a layer of fat on the top. Skim off the fat layer before using.

The stock will keep well chilled for a few days or freeze for up to 3 months.

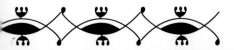

White chicken stock
Oilasko-salda argia
Caldo blanco de pollo

Ideal for rich comforting soups and rice dishes, white chicken stock is really versatile. Many supermarkets now sell authentic stocks but there's no substitute for a good homemade version, which will have a superior taste and clarity. For a well-developed flavour I like to use chicken wings but you can use any chicken bones – just make sure they're fresh. Washing the wings or bones before making the stock will remove some of the impurities and help create a clearer stock.

MAKES ABOUT 2 LITRES (3½ PINTS)
2 kg (4½ lb) chicken wings
2.5 litres (4½ pints) water
2 medium carrots, peeled and roughly chopped
2 large onions, peeled and roughly chopped
1 medium leek, white part only, roughly chopped
2 garlic cloves, peeled
1 bay leaf
2 sprigs of thyme

Rinse the chicken wings under cold running water then place in a stockpot and cover with the water. Place on the heat then bring to the boil. Turn down to a simmer, skimming any scum as it rises to the surface.

Add the vegetables and herbs then simmer gently for 4½ hours, removing any surface scum every 30 minutes. Remove from the heat and leave to rest for 15 minutes, before passing the stock through a fine sieve into a bowl. Discard the chicken, bones and vegetables. Let the stock cool before refrigerating. Once cold the stock will be quite gelatinous and have a layer of fat on the top. Skim off the fat layer before using.

The stock will keep chilled for a few days or frozen for up to 2 months.

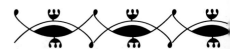

Vegetable stock
Barazki-salda
Caldo de verduras

It's always handy to have some vegetable stock in store in the fridge or freezer especially in winter as it's an essential base for many soups. I like to leave the vegetables to steep in the stock overnight before straining for a bit more flavour.

MAKES 2 LITRES (1¾ PINTS)
4 large onions, peeled and roughly chopped
4 large carrots, peeled and roughly chopped
4 celery sticks, roughly chopped
1 leek, rinsed and roughly chopped
2 garlic cloves, peeled
1 bay leaf
small handful parsley stalks
2 sprigs of thyme
10 black peppercorns
2.5 litres (4 ½ pints) water

Put the onion, carrot, celery and leek in a stockpot and cover with the water. Bring to the boil then reduce the heat to a simmer. Skim any scum from the surface, then add the garlic, herbs and peppercorns. Simmer gently for 45 minutes then remove from the heat and leave to cool. Once cold, pour through a fine sieve into a bowl and discard the vegetables. Pass through muslin (cheesecloth) then refrigerate for up to 3 days or freeze for up to 2 months.

Green mojo sauce
Mojo berdea
Mojo verde

Next time you grill any meat or fish, be sure to make some *mojo verde* to slather over the top before serving. Full of flavour, mojo verde complements grilled meats perfectly and is also suited to grilled fish, especially oily varieties like mackerel or sardines.

MAKES 300 ML (10½ FL OZ)
2 teaspoons cumin seeds
1 teaspoon salt
2 garlic cloves, peeled and finely chopped
250g (8oz) loosely packed flat leaf parsley
250g (8oz) loosely packed fresh coriander
1 small green chilli, roughly chopped
60 ml (2 fl oz) lemon juice
200 ml (7 fl oz) extra virgin olive oil

Toast the cumin seeds in a dry pan over medium-high heat for about 20 seconds or until aromatic. Using a mortar and pestle or an electric spice grinder, grind the cumin seeds with salt to a powder. Transfer to a food processor with the garlic, parsley, coriander leaves and chilli then pulse until smooth. Add the lemon juice and olive oil and pulse again until the mixture comes together.

Red mojo sauce
Mojo gorria
Mojo rojo

Originating in the Canary Islands mojo sauces are generally quite spicy and acidic. There are thousands of varieties, and the spiciness can vary from mild to extremely hot. They are usually

served at the start of the meal with bread, and are also commonly poured over *papas arrugadas*, a Canarian technique of cooking potatoes in sea water until they dry out and go wrinkly.

Mojo rojo with its balanced mix of spice, vinegar and sweetness works well with grilled meats. This recipe is quite mild so if you like it hotter, use hot paprika instead of the sweet variety, or blend in a fresh red chilli for a full spice kick.

MAKES 200 ML (7½ FL OZ)

1 red bell pepper (capsicum)
1 plum tomato
100 ml (3½ fl oz) extra virgin olive oil
1 teaspoon cumin seeds
1 garlic clove, peeled and finely chopped
½ teaspoon salt
½ teaspoon caster (superfine) sugar
1 teaspoon sweet paprika
1 teaspoon hot paprika
30 ml (2 tablespoons) white wine vinegar

Preheat the oven to 190°C/ 375°F/Gas mark 5.

Place the red pepper and tomato on a baking tray and drizzle with a little olive oil then bake for 20 minutes or until the skins start to blacken. Remove from the oven and place them in a small bowl covered tightly with cling film (plastic wrap). The vegetables will continue to steam, making it easy to remove the skin. Once cool enough to handle, slide the skin off the tomato and pepper and discard. Remove and discard the seeds from the pepper.

Toast the cumin seeds in a dry pan over medium-high heat for about 20 seconds or until aromatic, then, using a mortar and pestle, grind to a fine powder. Put the pepper, tomato, garlic, cumin, salt, sugar and paprikas in a food processor then purée until smooth. Add the vinegar and olive oil and pulse again until the mixture comes together.

Keep refrigerated for up to 4 days.

Mayonnaise
Maionesa
Mayonesa

Believed to have originated in the town of Mahon on the Spanish island of Menorca, this common condiment is popular throughout the world. Used on its own as a dressing for classics such as coleslaw and Russian salad, mayonnaise also makes a perfect base for other dressings like alioli.

If the emulsion separates or 'splits' at any time whisk the split mixture in a thin stream into another egg yolk to bring it back together.

MAKES 180 ML (6 FL OZ)
1 egg yolk
5 ml (1 teaspoon) white wine vinegar
5ml (1 teaspoon) cold water
¼ teaspoon fine sea salt
75 ml (5 tablespoons) vegetable oil
75 ml (5 tablespoons) light olive oil

In a mixing bowl, combine the egg yolk and white wine vinegar with 5 ml (1 teaspoon) water and salt and whisk until smooth. While still whisking slowly drizzle in the oils to create a smooth emulsion. If the mayonnaise is a little thick, whisk in a little more cold water

Alternatively, you can make mayonnaise in a food processor. Combine the yolk, vinegar, water and salt and then, with the motor running, slowly drizzle in the oils. Refrigerate in an airtight container.

Garlic mayonnaise
Alliolia
Alioli

Traditionally Spanish alioli is an emulsion of garlic and olive oil but often it results in an extremely garlicky experience, so I've lightened it. Don't hesitate to add more garlic if you prefer, but beware, the flavour will develop after it has rested for a while.

Alioli is a great accompaniment to meat and fish and raw or cooked vegetables all benefit from the addition of this wonderful garlicky sauce.

MAKES 180 ML (6 FL OZ)
1–3 garlic cloves, peeled, crushed to a paste with ¼ teaspoon coarse sea salt
1 egg yolk
5 ml (1 teaspoon) white wine vinegar
5 ml (1 teaspoon) water
75ml (5 tablespoons) vegetable oil
75ml (5 tablespoons) extra virgin olive oil

Put the crushed garlic in a bowl with the egg yolk, vinegar, water and salt then whisk to combine. Continue whisking while slowly drizzling in the oils to make an emulsion.

Whisk in more oil to thicken the emulsion or add water to thin it. The alioli will thicken considerably when refrigerated. Refrigerate in an airtight container.

For lemon alioli, replace the white wine vinegar with 30 ml (2 tablespoons) of lemon juice.

Sherry vinegar mayonnaise
Jerez-ozpin maionesa
Mayonesa de vinagre de jerez

The sherry vinegar in this mayonnaise really adds an interesting depth of flavour. It may not be as versatile as standard mayonnaise but it is delicious served with potatoes, cold meats and as a dressing for salads.

MAKES 200 ML (7 FL OZ)
1 garlic clove, peeled
¼ teaspoon fine sea salt
1 teaspoon Dijon mustard
1 egg yolk
15 ml (1 tablespoon) sherry vinegar
90 ml (3 fl oz) vegetable oil
90 ml (3 fl oz) extra virgin olive oil

Crush the garlic to a paste with the salt in a mortar and pestle or with the flat of a knife blade.

Place the Dijon mustard in a mixing bowl with the egg yolk, sherry vinegar, crushed garlic and salt, then whisk to combine. Continue whisking while slowly drizzling in the oils to make a smooth emulsion. You can speed up the addition of oil as you go but be careful not to add too much at a time or the mixture will split.

Sherry vinegar vinaigrette
Jerez ozpin-olioa
Vinagreta de jerez

I use this vinaigrette in all my salads. If you prefer you can use just olive or vegetable oil to make
this dressing but I like to mix the two to get a good balance of flavour, without it being too strong
and overpowering. Vinaigrettes refrigerate well but the oil will congeal when cold so bring to room
temperature and whisk well before serving.

MAKES 180 ML (6 FL OZ)
1 teaspoon Dijon mustard
¼ teaspoon fine salt
½ teaspoon caster (superfine) sugar
45 ml (3 tablespoons) sherry vinegar
15 ml (1 tablespoon) water
1 tablespoon finely chopped shallot
½ garlic clove, peeled and crushed
freshly ground black pepper
75 ml (5 tablespoons) extra virgin olive oil
75 ml (5 tablespoons) grape seed or vegetable oil

Whisk together the mustard, salt, sugar, sherry vinegar and water until smooth. Add the shallot,
garlic and freshly ground black pepper, then whisk in the oils to create a smooth emulsion.
Transfer to a screw-top jar and keep refrigerated.

Sherry vinaigrette separates so shake well or whisk before serving.

Bread and almond picada
Ogi eta almendra 'picada'
Picada de pan y almendras

A *picada* is thick paste commonly used in Catalan cooking. Added to wet dishes at the end of cooking a picada thickens and adds richness, along with another level of flavour. If you want to avoid using nuts in this recipe, simply replace with an extra tablespoon of breadcrumbs.

MAKES 50 G (2 OZ)
10 blanched almonds
15 ml (1 tablespoon) olive oil
2 tablespoons fresh breadcrumbs
½ garlic clove, peeled and crushed to a paste with ¼ teaspoon coarse sea salt
Small pinch saffron
15 ml (1 tablespoon) water

Heat a small frying pan over medium heat then add the blanched almonds and toast gently for about 30 seconds or until slightly golden and fragrant. Transfer to a bowl to cool. Return the pan to the heat and add the olive oil. Once hot, add the breadcrumbs and gently toast while stirring, until slightly golden. Tip the crumbs into the bowl with the almonds and leave to cool. Using a pestle and mortar pound the crushed garlic, saffron, almonds, breadcrumbs and water to a smooth paste. Alternatively, use a food processor.

Slow-cooked onions and peppers
Frijitukia
Sofrito

Used as a base for many Spanish dishes, *sofrito* is used in a similar way to tomato paste. The thick reduction of onion, pepper and tomato adds flavour to anything it's added to. Make a large batch and keep it in the refrigerator or freezer. After you discover how useful it is you'll always want some on hand.

MAKES ABOUT 120 G (4½ OZ)
45 ml (3 tablespoons) olive oil
2 garlic cloves, peeled and finely sliced
1 medium onion, peeled and finely diced
1 red bell pepper (capsicum), de-seeded and finely diced
½ teaspoon coarse sea salt
1 bay leaf
2 plum tomatoes, de-seeded and roughly chopped into small pieces

Heat the olive oil in a pan over medium heat. Add the garlic, onion, pepper and salt. Sauté while stirring for 5 minutes without colouring until the onion and pepper have softened. Reduce the heat and add the bay leaf. Continue cooking very gently for about 30 minutes, stirring occasionally to make sure the mixture doesn't stick to the pan. Stir in the chopped tomatoes and continue cooking slowly for another 45 minutes, stirring regularly. When cooked, the mixture will have a consistency like jam, and be a deep red-brown colour. Purée until smooth then pack in an airtight jar. Refrigerate until ready to use. Sofrito will keep for 1 week in the refrigerator or in the freezer for up to 3 months.

Romesco sauce
Romesko saltsa
Salsa romesco

Very popular all throughout Catalunya, *salsa romesco* is said to originate in the city of Tarragona just south of Barcelona. Typically an accompaniment to fish, Romesco is also commonly served with roasted *calçots*, a vegetable similar to a spring onion but difficult to find outside of Spain. It also works well with other grilled vegetables such as asparagus and leeks.

Every household has their own romesco recipe which they swear is the best, but they all include a mixture of nuts, peppers, garlic and olive oil. Dry *nora* peppers are usually used but they are still quite rare outside of Spain so I have replaced them with red bell peppers. The result is so similar, many of my Catalan friends can't tell the difference in flavour.

MAKES 250 ML (½ PINT)
1 red bell pepper (capsicum)
1 plum tomato
12 garlic cloves, skin left on
75 ml (5 tablespoons) extra virgin olive oil
5 cm (2 in) length of baguette, crust removed and torn into small pieces
30 g (1 oz) flaked almonds
1 teaspoon sweet paprika
1 teaspoon hot paprika
45 ml (3 tablespoons) sherry vinegar
Coarse sea salt

Preheat the oven to 190°C 375°F/ Gas mark 5.

Place the pepper, tomato and garlic on a baking try and drizzle with a little olive oil. Put into the hot oven and roast for 15 minutes. Remove the garlic from the tray and set aside. Continue roasting the pepper and tomato until the skins start to blacken and blister, about 10-15 minutes more. Remove from the oven and place in a small bowl covered tightly with cling film (plastic wrap). (It will continue to steam so the skin will slide off easily.) Once cool enough to handle,

skin and de-seed the pepper. Peel the skin off the tomato and squeeze the soft garlic from the skins then place both in a bowl with the flesh from the pepper.

Heat 15 ml (1 tablespoon) of the olive oil in a frying pan over medium heat. Add the bread and shaved almonds to the pan and sauté till golden and crisp. Leave to cool then put in the food processor and pulse till it resembles fine breadcrumbs. Add the pepper, tomato and garlic along with the paprikas and purée until smooth. Add the vinegar and remaining olive oil then pulse once more to bring the mixture together.

Season to taste with salt then transfer to a serving dish or refrigerate for up to 4 days.

Piquillo pepper sauce
Pikillo saltsa
Salsa de pimientos de piquillo

A speciality from the Navarre region of Spain, *pimientos de piquillo*, are a small red pepper, roasted over embers, which gives them a haunting smoky flavour, before being peeled and packed whole into cans or jars. The addition of smoked paprika in this sauce accentuates the flavour of the peppers, making it the perfect match to any red meat, chicken or even a breakfast of fried morcilla and eggs.

MAKES ABOUT 300 ML (10 FL OZ)
15 ml (1 tablespoon) light olive oil
1 garlic clove, peeled and finely sliced
1 small onion, peeled and diced
1 teaspoon smoked paprika
2 plum tomatoes, roughly chopped
200 g (7 oz) piquillo peppers, drained, halved and seeds scraped out
30 ml (2 tablespoons) white wine vinegar

1 tablespoon caster (superfine) sugar
Coarse sea salt

Heat the olive oil in a small pan over medium heat. Add the garlic and sauté until lightly golden. Add the onion and smoked paprika then continue cooking until soft and translucent. Add the tomatoes, then continue cooking until reduced and pulpy, about 10–15 minutes. Roughly chop the peppers then add to the pan along with the vinegar and sugar.

Bring to a simmer then reduce the heat to low and leave the sauce to reduce for about 5 minutes. Transfer the sauce to a food processor and blend till smooth. If it looks too dry add a little water to loosen it, it should be the same consistency of tomato ketchup. Pass through a fine sieve and season to taste with salt before packing into a bottle or airtight container. Piquillo pepper sauce keeps well chilled for about 1 week.

Preparing baby globe artichokes
Orburuak
Alcachofas

Preparing baby artichokes is fiddly but worth the effort as they have a superior flavour to the canned variety, which can be quite acidic and lack flavour. Use canned artichokes if you're short of time but rinse off the brine and leave them to drain thoroughly first. These artichokes are great served with a drizzle of vinaigrette and are used in some of the dishes in this book.

5 baby artichokes
1 lemon, halved
1 garlic clove, peeled
1 bay leaf
2 sprigs of thyme
3 black peppercorns

½ teaspoon salt
100 ml (3½ fl oz) white wine
800 ml (1½ pints) water

Pull the outer leaves from the artichokes and discard. Use a serrated knife to cut the top off the artichoke and trim the stem to about 2.5 cm (1 in). With a small sharp knife, trim off the outer layer of the stem then run it around the outer circumference to remove the remaining leaves.

Using a teaspoon, scoop out the fibres from inside the head of the artichoke. Use a lemon half to wipe juice over the artichoke to stop it from going brown.

Repeat with the other artichokes then place in a pan.

Squeeze the juice of the other lemon half over the artichokes. Add the garlic, bay leaf, thyme, peppercorns, salt, wine and water to a pan. Place over a medium heat then bring to a gentle simmer. Cook gently for 12–15 minutes or until tender. Test by pricking with a skewer, it should pass through the artichoke easily. Remove from the heat and leave to cool in the liquid. Refrigerate in the liquid until ready to use, or serve cold with a drizzle of vinaigrette.

Preparing dried chickpeas
Txitxirioak
Garbanzo

MAKES 250 G (9 OZ)
3½ oz (100 g) chickpeas
½ large onion, peeled
½ large carrot peeled
1 stick celery, cut into 4
1 bay leaf

Put the chickpeas in a large pot and cover with 1 litre (1¾ pints) of cold water. Allow to soak in the refrigerator for 12–24 hours.

Drain and rinse in cold water. Return to the pot, cover generously with water then add the onion, carrot, celery and bay leaf. Bring to the boil over a high heat, reduce heat to a simmer and cook for 1–1½ hours or until soft. Cooking time can vary so keep an eye on the chickpeas to make sure they don't dry out. You may need to add more water during cooking. When cooked, pour into a colander to drain, and discard the onion, carrot, celery and bay leaf.

Preparing lentils
Dilistak
Lentejas

MAKES 400 G (14 OZ)
200 g (7 oz) small green Puy or brown lentils
½ medium onion, peeled and cut in half
    (keep the root end intact so the onion doesn't fall apart while cooking)
1 medium carrot, peeled and cut in half lengthways
1 celery stick, cut into 4
1 clove garlic, peeled
1 bay leaf
sea salt

Bring 2 litres (3½ pints) water to the boil in a pan, and add the lentils, onion, carrot, celery, garlic and bay leaf. Reduce the heat to a simmer and cook gently for about 15 minutes, adding a good sprinkling of sea salt. Cook for another 10 minutes, or until the lentils are tender. When ready they should be soft but not falling apart. Pour into a colander or sieve to drain. Remove and discard the vegetables and bay leaf.

Preparing dried beans
Babarrunak
Alubias

MAKES ABOUT 250 G (9 OZ)
3 ½ oz (100 g) dried beans
1 bay leaf
½ large onion, peeled
1 celery stalk
½ large carrot, peeled

COOKING TIMES
CANELLINI   45–55 MINS
BUTTER   60–75 MINS

Place the beans in a large pan and cover with 1 litre (1¾ pints) of cold water. Leave to soak in the refrigerator for 12–24 hours.

Drain the beans and rinse in cold water. Place back in the pot, cover with another 2 litres (3½ pints) of water and bring to a boil over high heat. Boil vigorously for 10 minutes, reduce the heat to a simmer, skimming any froth off the surface and discarding it. Add the bay leaf, onion, celery and carrot and cook for the specified time, or until soft but not completely falling apart. Check occasionally while simmering as cooking times can vary. Pour into a colander to drain then discard the onion, carrot and celery and bay leaf.

Preparing salt cod
Arrain-kontserba
Conservar el pescado

300 g (10 oz) cod fillet, skinned and pin boned
100 g (3½ oz) coarse sea salt
50 g (1 ¾ oz) fine sea salt

Rinse the fillet under cold running water and pat dry with kitchen paper. Put a length of absorbent kitchen paper, long enough to wrap the fillet, on a tray and make a bed in the middle with half the salt. Place the fillet on top and cover the fillet with the remaining salt. Carefully wrap into a tight package and place onto a wire rack sitting on a tray or plate, to catch the juices. Place in the fridge and leave for 24 hours, turning after 12 hours. Remove the paper, rinse the fillet under cold running water and pat dry with kitchen paper. By now the cod will have lost a lot of liquid and be quite firm. Roll the fillet in the fine sea salt till completely coated and place on a clean wire rack and return to the fridge. Leave the cod to dry, uncovered, for another 5 days or more before using.

   Bacalao needs to be soaked in cold water to extract the salt and rehydrate the flesh before cooking so you will need to plan ahead for this.

Preparing salt cod for cooking
Bakailao gazituaren prestakuntza
Preparación del Bacalao salado

Rinse any visible salt off the cod, place in a large pan and cover with cold water. Place in the fridge and leave to soak for 24 hours for each 2.5 cm (1 in) thickness in flesh, changing the water every 6 hours or so.

SOUP

Zopak

SOPA

I LOVE PREPARING SOUPS and here I have included some of my favourites, influenced by the flavours of Spain and the Basque Country. Each region has its own soups that match the climate perfectly. From the famous cooling *gazpachos* and *solmorejos* from the south to the warming *caldos* and *porrusalda* to the North, soups feature heavily in Spanish cuisine. Coastal areas make the most of seafood in soups such as the *Basque sopa de pescado* while the central areas of the country make the most of economical, readily available ingredients such as bread, garlic and paprika, such as in the humble *sopa de ajo* from the Castillian region of Spain.

When making soups at home I love to play around with different garnishes to give extra flavour and contrast in texture which adds interest to every bite (or slurp).

Almond gazpacho with oloroso sherry

'Ajo blanco' oloroso jerezarekin

Ajo blanco con oloroso de jerez

Almonds are used extensively in Spain particularly in the south where *ajo blanco* is a popular soup most commonly served with grapes and, sometimes quite bizarrely, baked potatoes. I like to get a little playful with the classics, as in this instance, by occasionally serving my ajo blanco topped with a sprinkling of sweet oloroso sherry jelly. The sweet sherry works well with the creamy soup. Try to get the soup as smooth as possible in a food processor or blender to purée it and don't force it through a sieve or it will have an unpleasant gritty texture. Serve it ice cold as in the south of Spain.

Almond gazpacho with oloroso sherry

SERVES 4

150 g (5 oz) fresh white bread, crust removed
300 g (10 oz) blanched almonds
1 litre (1¾ pints) water
1 garlic clove, peeled
120 ml (4 fl oz) extra virgin olive oil, plus extra for drizzling
15 ml (1 tablespoon) white wine vinegar
Coarse sea salt

OLOROSO JELLY
½ leaf gelatine
100 ml (3½ fl oz) oloroso sherry
½ teaspoon caster (superfine) sugar

Tear the bread into bite-sized chunks and place in a bowl with the almonds. Pour over the water, cover and refrigerate overnight.

Place the gelatine leaf in a bowl and pour in enough cold water to cover. Set aside to soak. Pour the sherry into a small pan, add the sugar and gently heat while stirring until the sugar has dissolved. Drain the gelatine and squeeze out any water then add to the warm sherry. Stir until dissolved then remove from the heat and leave to cool, but not set. Pour the jelly into another bowl, then cover and refrigerate overnight.

The next day put the soaked gazpacho mixture into a food processor with the garlic, olive oil and white wine vinegar. Purée for a few minutes until smooth, then pour through a fine sieve into a bowl. Stir but don't force the solids through. Discard any solids left in the sieve. Season the soup with a little salt to taste. Chill the soup for a couple of hours until it's really cold before serving.

To serve, divide between four chilled bowls. Scoop the jelly out of the bowl and chop roughly then scatter over the soup. Finish with a little drizzle of olive oil.

Garlic and paprika soup with poached egg

Baratxuri zopa arraultzarekin

Sopa de ajo con huevo escalfado

Originally prepared by shepherds during their long treks through Castilla La Mancha, *sopa de ajo* is now eaten all over Spain. The most basic version is made from water, garlic, pepper and bread, and the dish has now evolved into a number of regional varieties. In the south, paprika is used, while in the north, a dried pepper called *choricero* is more common, while some regions in the south even add cauliflower.

I like the basic version best with the addition of an egg, which is common in all regions. The only difference here is that I like to blend the soup to make it a bit more refined, but most Spaniards would probably scoff at that idea. Leave it chunky if you want, and don't worry about the soup being too garlicky, the cooking time makes it turn sweet and not too strong.

SᴇRVES 4

45 ml (3 tablespoons) mild olive oil
12 garlic cloves, peeled and cut in half
100 g (3½ oz) stale white bread, torn into small pieces
½ small onion, finely chopped
2 teaspoons sweet paprika
1 teaspoon hot paprika
1 litre (1¾ pints) white chicken stock
4 eggs
30 ml (2 tablespoons) white wine vinegar (optional)
1 litre (1¾ pints) of water
Coarse sea salt

Heat the olive oil in a pan over medium heat. Add the garlic cloves and cook until a deep golden colour on all sides, stirring constantly. Using a slotted spoon, remove the garlic from the pan and set to one side.

Return the pan back to the heat and add the bread. Cook while stirring until golden and crisp. Remove 2 tablespoons of the crisp bread from the pan and reserve for garnishing. Add the onion to the pan with the bread and sweat down until soft.

Add the cooked garlic and paprikas and stir to combine. Pour over the stock and simmer for 15 minutes or until the garlic is soft enough to crush.

Pour the soup into a blender and purée until smooth then pass through a fine sieve using the back of a spoon to work it through. Add salt to taste then pour back into a pan and place over a low heat to keep warm.

Meanwhile, pour the water and vinegar into another small pan and bring to a simmer. Crack the eggs into the water and poach until the whites are set, but the yolk is still runny, about 3–3½ minutes. Use a slotted spoon to transfer to four warm bowls. Pour the soup around the eggs then sprinkle over the reserved crisp bread.

Cauliflower soup with crisp garlic and toasted almonds

Azalore-krema baratxuri kurruskaria eta

almendra txigortuekin

Crema de coliflor con ajo crujiente y almendras tostadas

Cauliflower has made a resurgence in popularity in the culinary scene recently. It makes the most amazing soup with a creamy, almost velvety texture. Any smooth soup works well with a nice crunchy contrast in texture such as croutons. To give this soup an interesting flavour as well as texture, I've added a mix of crisp bread, garlic and almond to sprinkle over the top. The flavours work wonderfully together, and the garlicky bread and almonds cut into the creamy soup perfectly.

Cauliflower soup with crisp garlic and toasted almonds

SERVES 4

30 ml (2 tablespoons) light olive oil

2 garlic cloves, peeled and sliced

7 cm (3 in) piece of leek, white part only, rinsed and finely chopped

1 small onion, peeled and diced

300 g (10 oz) cauliflower, cut into small pieces

600 ml (1¼ pints) vegetable stock

Coarse sea salt

GARNISH

30 ml (2 tablespoons) mild olive oil

2 garlic cloves, finely sliced

5 cm (2 in) chunk of baguette, torn into bite-sized cubes

2 tablespoons flaked almonds

Small handful flat leaf parsley

Heat the olive oil in a pan over medium heat, then add the garlic and gently sauté till aromatic. Add the leek and onion to the pan. Cover and allow to sweat, stirring regularly until the onion is soft and translucent, about 5 minutes. Add the cauliflower and replace the cover. Continue to cook slowly for another 5 minutes, stirring occasionally so that the vegetables don't stick to the base of the pan.

Pour in the stock and heat to a gentle simmer. Cook until the cauliflower is soft (about 4–5 minutes, depending on its size). Transfer to a blender and purée until smooth.

Use a rubber spatula to work the soup through a fine sieve into a clean pan. Season to taste with salt then place over a low heat to keep warm while preparing the garnish.

To make the garnish, heat the olive oil in a small frying pan over low heat then add the garlic. Cook slowly while shaking the pan until the garlic is golden and crisp. Use a slotted spoon to remove the garlic from the pan and place on kitchen paper. Return the pan to the heat and re-heat the oil over a medium heat. Add bread cubes and almonds. Sauté while constantly shaking the pan till the bread and almonds are golden and crisp then transfer to the ktichen paper with the garlic. Once the mix has cooled, put in a small bowl with the chopped parsley and stir to combine.

Divide the soup between four warmed bowls then scatter over the crisp garnish.

Courgette soup with cream cheese and basil

Kuiatxo-krema gazta krematsu eta albakarekin

Crema de calabacín con queso cremoso y albahaca

At the end of summer when the days start to shorten I quite often make this soup when the courgettes are at their best. Basil works really well with courgette and is usually in season at the same time. I like to blend a few leaves into the soup at the end of cooking, which gives it a lovely taste and aroma. The cream cheese adds a little sourness and creaminess. Once the cream cheese has been added just make sure the soup doesn't boil again or it will separate and leave white specks all through your lovely green soup.

Serves 4

30 ml (2 tablespoons) light olive oil, plus extra to serve
1 small onion, peeled and diced
1 garlic clove, peeled and finely chopped
1 small baking potato, about 150 g (5 oz), peeled and grated
300 g (10 oz) courgette (zucchini), finely chopped
550 ml (1 pint) vegetable stock
10 basil leaves
55 g (2 oz) cream cheese
Coarse sea salt

Heat the olive oil in a pan over a medium heat. Add the onion and garlic, and sweat down until soft without colouring. Add the grated potato and continue cooking for another 5 minutes or until soft.

Increase the heat and add the courgette and vegetable stock. Bring to the boil then reduce the heat to a simmer and leave to cook for 10 minutes, or until the courgette is soft.

Remove the pan from the heat and set aside for 5 minutes to cool a little. When cooled, add the basil leaves. Pour the soup into a blender and purée for a few minutes until smooth. Season to taste with coarse sea salt.

To make the soup really smooth and silky use a rubber spatula to work it through a fine sieve. Pour back into the pan and whisk in the cream cheese.

Serve with a drizzle of olive oil and some good bread or croutons.

Basque fish and shellfish soup

Arrai eta itsaski zopa

Sopa de pescado y marisco a la vasca

This soup and others very similar are common all along the Basque coast of Spain, and are served up in most restaurants and homes. Each version contains a good mix of the fabulous seafood caught from the cold Cantabrian sea.

You could make this soup with just a few types of seafood but the combination of molluscs, shellfish and finfish really give it an amazing flavour and also make it visually stunning. *Sopa de pescado y marisco a la vasca* is often thickened with bread but flour is also quite common, and gives it a smoother, creamier texture.

Basque fish and shellfish soup

SERVES 4

30 ml (2 tablespoons) mild olive oil

12 king prawns, heads and shells removed and reserved
    (leave the tails on for presentation)

3 garlic cloves, peeled and finely sliced

1 medium onion, peeled and finely diced

1 medium carrot, peeled and finely diced

5 cm (2 in) length leek, white part only, rinsed and finely chopped

4 plum tomatoes, seeds removed and roughly chopped

Small handful flat leaf parsley leaves, shredded

150 ml (5 fl oz) white wine

2 tablespoons plain (all-purpose) flour

600 ml (1 pint) fish stock

200 g (7 oz) monkfish, cut into 1 cm (½ in) thick medallions

12 mussels, de-bearded and rinsed

12 clams, purged (see Pantry)

Heat half the olive oil in a pan over medium heat. Add the prawn shells and heads to the pan and fry until bright red and aromatic. Add the garlic, onion, carrot and leek to the pan and allow to sweat down for 8–10 minutes or until the vegetables are soft and starting to colour a little. Add the chopped tomatoes and parsley to the pan and continue cooking until the tomatoes break down to a thick pulp, about 10 minutes.

Pour in the white wine and simmer until completely reduced, then sprinkle over the flour and stir to thoroughly combine. Pour the fish stock over the mixture while whisking to stop lumps forming then bring to a simmer and cook gently for 10 minutes. Pass the soup through a fine sieve prressing with the back of a spoon to extract as much flavour and liquid as possible. Discard the solids.

Heat the remaining olive oil in a pan big enough to hold the soup. Add the prawns and fish pieces to the hot oil and sear for 3 seconds on each side (it doesn't matter if the fish is not cooked through as it will be finished in the soup). Remove the fish and prawns from the pan and set aside. Pour the soup back into the pan.

Bring the soup back to a simmer then add the mussels and clams. Cook for 3–5 minutes until all the shells have opened. Discard any shells that don't open, then add the prawns and fish back to the soup. Simmer for another minute then remove from the heat. The soup shouldn't need any salt as the shellfish are quite salty but add some to taste if needed.

Divide the fish and shellfish between four warm bowls then pour over the soup.

Parsnip veloute with burnt butter hazelnuts and fresh apple

Txiribi-krema gurin errea, hur eta sagarrarekin

Crema de chirivía con mantequilla quemada, avellana y manzana

An underused vegetable in my opinion, parsnip makes an outstanding winter soup, full of earthy sweet flavour with a beautiful luscious and creamy texture. Finely chopped apple adds more sweetness and an extra textural contrast while the toasted hazelnut butter adds a welcome saltiness. This really is a great soup and goes to show how humble ingredients can be transformed into something special.

SERVES 4

40 g (1½ oz) shelled hazelnuts
30 ml (2 tablespoons) mild olive oil
1 medium onion, peeled and diced
2 garlic cloves, peeled and sliced
300 g (10 oz) parsnip, peeled and roughly diced
600 ml (1 pint) vegetable stock
100 ml (3½ fl oz) milk
50 g (1¾ oz) butter
½ granny smith apple
Coarse sea salt

Preheat the oven to 180°C/350°F/Gas mark 4.

Spread the hazelnuts on a baking tray and toast in the oven for 7–8 minutes or until a light golden colour then set aside to cool. Once cool, tip into a plastic bag, then using a rolling pin coarsely crush them and set aside.

Heat the olive oil in a pan over medium heat. Add the onion and garlic and cook until soft and translucent. Add the parsnip, cover, and cook for 6–7 minutes stirring regularly to stop the vegetables sticking to the base of the pan. Add the stock, cover, and simmer gently for another 8–10 minutes or until the parsnip is soft enough to crush with the back of a fork. Remove from the heat and leave to cool for 5 minutes. Pour parsnip mixture into a blender and purée until smooth. Pass through a fine sieve to make it extra smooth then stir in the milk and add salt to taste.

Place over a low heat to keep warm.

Meanwhile melt the butter in a small pan over medium heat then turn the heat up a bit and stir until butter starts to brown. Remove from the heat and pour into a glass bowl to stop the butter cooking. Add the chopped hazelnuts then finely slice the apples and cut into matchsticks.

Divide the soup between four warm bowls then drizzle with hazelnut butter. Sprinkle over the apple batons and serve.

Basque potato and leek soup with salt cod buñuelos and alioli

Porrusalda bakailao-kausera eta alioliarekin

Porrusalda con buñuelos de bacalao y alioli

Porrusalda is a simple Basque dish of potato and leek cooked together into a thick soupy stew. It's commonly served with the addition of salt cod for added flavour. Instead of mixing the cod through the soup, in this dish they are made into crunchy fritters or *buñuelos*, which adds an interesting element to the dish. The garlicky alioli brings the two main elements together perfectly adding richness and another layer of flavour.

This is quite a long recipe so you might want to save it for a special occasion or leave out the buñuelos and simply flake poached cod over the top to make it a little simpler. As with other soups, this porrusalda is smooth but it also works well when left chunky, just make sure to dice the vegetables finely before cooking.

Basque potato and leek soup with salt cod buñuelos and alioli

SERVES 4

15 ml (1 tablespoon) olive oil
1 garlic clove, peeled and finely chopped
200 g (7 oz) leek, white part only, washed and diced
½ small onion, peeled and diced
1 stick of celery, diced
1 bay leaf
1 medium baking potato, (about 200 g/7 oz) peeled and finely diced
300 ml (10 fl oz) vegetable stock
300 ml (10 fl oz) milk
Coarse sea salt

BUÑUELOS

120 g (4¼ oz) salt cod, desalinated, see pantry
60 ml (2 fl oz) water
15 ml (1 tablespoon) olive oil
Sea salt
15 g (½ oz) butter
35 g (1 ½ oz) plain (all-purpose) flour
1 egg

TO FINISH

30 ml (2 tablespoons) milk
80 ml (2¾ fl oz) alioli
Vegetable oil for frying (at least 1 litre/1¾ pints)
Small bunch of chives, finely chopped

To make the soup, heat the olive oil in a pan over medium heat and add the garlic. Gently sauté until slightly golden and aromatic. Add the leek, onion, celery and bay leaf to the pan, cover, and sweat down, stirring occasionally until the onion is soft and translucent, about 5 minutes.

Add the potato to the pan and cover with a lid. Continue to cook slowly for another 5 minutes, stirring occasionally so that the potato doesn't stick to the base of the pan. Pour in the stock and simmer gently until the potato is soft, about 10–12 minutes. Remove the bay leaf and transfer the soup to a blender. Pour in the milk, then season to taste and purée until smooth.

To make the soup really smooth, pass the mixture through a fine sieve using a rubber spatula to force it through.

To make the buñuelos, bring a small pan of water to the boil and add the prepared salt cod [See Pantry]. Bring it back to the boil, then remove the pan from the heat and allow to steep for 5 minutes.

Drain the cod and rinse under cold water. When cool enough to handle, remove and discard the skin. Flake the cod, making sure to remove any bones, then roughly chop into small pieces and set aside. Put the water, olive oil, salt and butter into a small pan and bring to a simmer over medium heat. As soon as the butter has melted add all the flour then stir briskly with a wooden spoon till the mixture comes together. Keep beating the mixture for another 30 seconds then remove the pan from the heat and leave to cool for a minute. Add the egg and beat vigorously till the mixture comes together and is smooth and shiny, then fold in the salt cod until well incorporated.

To finish, whisk the milk into the alioli. It should be the consistency of double (heavy) cream so add a bit more milk if necessary.

Pour the vegetable oil in a pan (or use a fryer if you have one) and heat to 185°C/365°F. Use a sugar thermometer to check the temperature or drop a small piece of white bread in the oil, it should be golden brown in about 30 seconds.

Meanwhile, put the soup in a pan over a medium heat to warm, making sure not to boil it.

Dip two teaspoons in the oil so the mixture slides off easily. Working quickly, scoop up a spoon of the mixture then shape with the other spoon and drop into the hot oil. Repeat till you have 10 buñuelos. Cook for 1 minute or until golden and crisp then transfer to paper towel to soak up any excess oil.

Repeat with the rest of the mix until you have 20 buñuelos in total.

Divide the soup between the bowls then top each with five buñuelos, or serve on the side if you prefer. Drizzle with the alioli and sprinkle over the chives.

Cold tomato and bread soup with crab, chilli and avocado

Salmorejoa txangurro eta ahuakatearekin

Salmorejo con cangrejo y aguacate

Very similar to gazpacho but even simpler to make, *salmorejo* is a cold soup best served in late summer when the tomatoes are full of juicy sweetness and the days are still hot. In the south of Spain salmorejo is served quite thick, almost like a dip in some cases then garnished with boiled eggs and jamón, but this version is a little lighter and more refreshing. Crab is a perfect garnish for salmorejo and a little kick of chilli really livens it up. Salmorejo relies on good ingredients so make sure to use the ripest tomatoes you can and a good olive oil to drizzle over the top.

Cold tomato and bread soup with crab, chilli and avocado

SERVES 4

100 g (3½ oz) stale white bread, crusts removed and torn into pieces
150 ml (5 fl oz) water
800 g (1¾ lb) very ripe plum tomatoes
1 garlic clove, peeled and sliced
60 ml (2 fl oz) extra virgin olive oil, plus a little extra for drizzling
15 ml (1 tablespoon) white wine vinegar
1 teaspoon coarse sea salt
100 g (3½ oz) fresh crab meat
*1 small red chilli, finely chopped (remove the seeds if you
     don't want it too spicy)*
1 small avocado

Put the bread in a small bowl and cover with the water to soak for 10 minutes. Meanwhile, place the tomatoes and garlic in a food processor and purée for a minute or until as smooth as possible. Pass the tomato purée through a fine sieve, pushing with the back of a spoon to extract as much liquid as possible. Discard the solids then pour the tomato liquid back into the food processor. Add the soaked bread, olive oil, vinegar and salt, then purée for another minute or until smooth. Pass through a fine sieve making sure to press with the back of a spoon to get as much liquid as possible. Check the seasoning and add more if needed, then put in the refrigerator to chill until very cold.

Meanwhile, prepare the crab. Pick through the crab with your fingertips to remove any small pieces of shell, then place in a small bowl. Add the chilli and a pinch of salt, then stir to combine.

To serve, divide the soup between four chilled bowls. Peel the avocado then finely dice and sprinkle it over the soup. Scatter over the crab and drizzle with a little extra virgin olive oil.

Pancetta, broad bean and chicken broth with fideo

Oilasko salda hirugihar, baba eta fideoekin

Caldo de pollo con panceta, habas y fideos

Hearty, warming and comforting, it's no wonder noodle soups are popular around the world and, of course, Spain has its own version. The Catalan dish *fideua* is similar to paella but made with pasta instead of rice. *Fideo* noodles are also perfect for soups and broths such as this. *Caldos* in Spain can be served with any combination of ingredients but usually pork or chicken are involved, along with vegetables such as cabbage or broad beans. If you cant find fideo noodles replace them with any type of long, thin pasta. Simply wrap them in a clean tea towel then run it over the edge of a bench while pulling down firmly at each end to snap the pasta into short pieces.

Pancetta, broad bean and chicken broth with fideo

SERVES 4

15 ml (1 tablespoon) olive oil
8 chicken drumsticks
100 g (3 ½ oz) pancetta, cut into small dice
2 garlic cloves, peeled and finely sliced
1 medium onion, peeled and finely diced
1 medium carrot, peeled and finely diced
1 celery stalk, finely diced
1 litre (1¾ pints) of water

1 bay leaf
2 sprigs of thyme
2 sprigs of parsley
200 g (7 oz) broad (fava) beans, shelled
100 g (3½ oz) fine fideo
Coarse sea salt
Extra virgin olive oil, for drizzling

Heat the olive oil in a large pan over medium heat. Add the chicken drumsticks and sear on all sides until golden. Add the pancetta and continue cooking while stirring until the fat is released and the pancetta is starting to crisp. Add the garlic, onion, carrot and celery and allow the vegetables to sweat for a few minutes without colouring.

Pour over the water then add the bay leaf, thyme and parsley. Bring to a simmer and cook for 25 minutes then remove from the heat. Pick out and discard the herbs. Use a slotted spoon to remove the drumsticks from the broth and set aside.

Once cool enough to handle, remove the flesh from the bone and shred into small pieces, discarding the skin and bones. Skim any excess fat from the top of the broth, then add the shredded chicken. Place the broth back on the heat then add the broad beans and fideo. Bring back to a simmer and cook for 5 minutes or until the fideo is *al dente*. Check the seasoning and add a little salt if needed.

Serve immediately with crusty bread and a drizzle of extra virgin olive oil.

TAPAS & PINTXOS

TAPAS & PINTXOS

TAPAS AND PINTXOS ARE A WAY OF LIFE IN SPAIN. The traditional Spanish tapa is thought to have originated in the taverns of Andalusia where drinks, more often than not sherry, would be served with a slice of bread over the glass to stop annoying fruit flies from falling in. The word *tapa*, which translates as 'cover' now refers to just about any small snack or plate served with drinks, usually between the main meals of the day, in the afternoon.

Tapas evolved first with the addition of a slice of ham or chorizo or something else salty to support the clientele's thirst. As their popularity grew the creations became more elaborate and sophisticated and these days many tapa bars will employ highly skilled chefs to prepare the daily offerings.

Pintxos, the Basque name for tapas, are taken extremely seriously and prestigious annual competitions pit chefs against each other to create the best pintxo with the winners receiving almost celebrity recognition. Pintxos differ from tapas in that traditionally most are spiked with a skewer to hold them together or to keep them attached to the bread they are served on.

I suggest making four varieties of tapas and pintxos to serve as a light meal for four people. The larger the variety you prepare the more interesting the meal will be.

Ham croquettes

Urdaiazpiko kroketak

Croquetas de jamón

I've eaten hundreds of croquettes during my visits to Spain and have experimented with different recipes to try to reproduce them. These are a 'best of' version combining the best of what I've tried and they are truly gorgeous. They do take a bit of work as well as chilling time to set so you will need to plan ahead but you can make them up to a few days before eating, then store in the refrigerator before frying.

I like to use Japanese panko breadcrumbs for my croquettes for an extra light and crisp shell. You do need to blitz them to a powder beforehand though. Panko is naturally very course so unless blitzed, they won't make a proper seal and the béchamel may leak when frying the croquettes.

Ham croquettes

Makes 18

500 ml (1 pint) milk
½ bay leaf
¼ small onion, peeled and roughly chopped
¼ teaspoon grated nutmeg
50 g (1¾ oz) butter
30 ml (2 tablespoons) olive oil
100 g (3½ oz) jamón serrano, diced
55 g (2 oz) plain (all-purpose) flour
1 tablespoon cornflour (cornstarch)
Fine sea salt

TO FINISH
100 g (3½ oz) plain (all-purpose) flour
2 eggs, beaten
75 g (2½ oz) Panko breadcrumbs, pulsed in a food processor to a powder
1 litre (1¾ pints) vegetable oil, for deep frying

Place the milk, bay leaf, onion and nutmeg in a small pan, over a medium heat. As soon as the milk comes to a simmer remove from the heat and leave to steep.

Meanwhile, in another pan, melt the butter with the olive oil over a low heat. Add the diced jamón and gently cook for 3 minutes to render out the fat. Sprinkle the flours over, then stir to combine into a thick paste. Gently cook while stirring for 5 minutes making sure the flour doesn't stick to the base of the pan. Set aside.

Pass the milk through a fine sieve and discard the solids. Return the jamón roux to the heat and whisk in a quarter of the milk.

Continue whisking while slowly pouring in the remaining milk until smooth. Don't add the milk too fast or you may end up with lumps. Bring the mixture to a gentle simmer while scraping the bottom of the pan with a rubber spatula to make sure it doesn't catch. Continue to cook gently for 15 minutes, stirring occasionally. Season the mixture to taste with fine sea salt, then transfer to a tray. Cover with cling film (plastic wrap) and refrigerate until firm, about 3 hours.

To finish the croquettes, place the flour, beaten egg and panko in three separate bowls. Measure out 2 tablespoons of the mixture, then with floured hands, roll into a ball and form into a cylinder about 5 cm (2 in) long. Dust in flour, then dip into the egg, shake off any excess and then place the croquette in the breadcrumbs to coat. Spread out on a tray and repeat with the remaining mixture until you have 18 croquettes. At this stage you can refrigerate the croquettes and cook them later.

To cook the croquettes, heat the vegetable oil in a pan or deep fryer and heat to 180°C/355°F. If you don't have a fryer use a sugar thermometer to check the temperature or drop a small piece of white bread in the oil; it should be golden brown after 30 seconds. Fry the croquettes six at a time until golden and crisp then place on a paper towel to absorb any excess oil. Serve while hot.

Salt cod in olive oil and garlic emulsion

Bakailaoa pil-pil erara

Bacalao al pil pil

Probably one of the most typical Basque dishes of all, *bacalao al pil pil* is a perfect example of what I love about the cooking of this region. Take a few humble ingredients, combine with a genius technique and the result is something magnificent. By slowly shaking the pan while cooking, the natural gelatine from the salt cod mixes into the olive oil creating an amazingly light emulsified sauce. I admit though, it's not the easiest dish to master but if the sauce fails to emulsify in the pan simply tip it into a warm bowl and give a good whisk until it comes together.

Salt cod in olive oil and garlic emulsion

SERVES 4

1 large floury potato, about 200 g/7 oz, peeled and cut into 4 thick slices
100 ml (3½ fl oz) extra virgin olive oil
2 garlic cloves, peeled and finely sliced
1 dried red chilli, seeds removed and sliced
250 g (9 oz) salt cod loin, desalinated (see Pantry)
*   cut into 4 even pieces*
Small handful flat leaf parsley, finely chopped
Coarse sea salt

Put the potato slices in a small pan of salted water and bring to a simmer and cook until tender. Drain in a colander.

Heat the olive oil in a non-stick frying pan over a low heat then add the garlic and chilli. Gently fry, shaking the pan until the garlic is golden and crisp. Remove the garlic from the oil and place on kitchen paper. Leave the pan off the heat to cool slightly, then return to a low heat.

Add the cod to the pan, skin side down, and gently shake the pan so the cod slides around in the oil. As it cooks it will start to emulsify the olive oil.

Continue cooking, shaking the pan for 7–8 minutes or until the cod is half cooked and the olive oil is emulsified. Carefully turn the cod over and continue cooking in the same manner on the other side for another 5–6 minutes, or until cooked through. The cod is cooked when it starts to flake when pressed.

Place the potatoes in the pan to warm through then transfer to a serving dish and sprinkle the parsley over the top. Carefully lift the cod from the sauce and place a piece on top of each potato disc. If the sauce hasn't fully emulsified pour into a mixing bowl and give it a good whisk to bring it together. Pour the sauce over the cod then garnish with the reserved crisp garlic and chilli.

Calamari with fried garlic, chilli and lemon alioli

Txibiak baratxuri, txile eta limoi allioliarekin

Calamares con ajo frito, chile y alioli de limón

Some of the best fried calamari I've ever tasted was in San Sebastian in the north of Spain. Tiny calamari or *chipirones*, barely an inch long are dusted in the lightest coating then fried to crispy perfection. My version is very light, crisp and not at all oily – just as fried calamari should be. For the best results, make sure the oil is clean and at the right temperature before frying. The addition of fried garlic and chilli adds a little extra kick to the recipe, but omit it if you prefer.

Calamari with fried garlic, chilli and lemon alioli

SERVES 4

3 small squid, weighing about 120 g (4 oz) each
50 g (1¾ oz) cornflour (cornstarch)
50 g (1¾ oz) self-raising (self-rising) flour
50 g (1¾ oz) fine white corn maize (see Pantry)
½ teaspoon fine sea salt
4 garlic cloves, peeled and finely sliced
2 small red chilli, de-seeded and thinly sliced
Vegetable oil, for frying (at least 1 litre/1 ¾ pints)
180 ml (6 fl oz) lemon alioli (see Basics)
Coarse sea salt

To prepare the squid, pull the head and tentacles away from the body, which will come away quite easily. Cut the part of the head with the eyes off and discard. In the centre where the tentacles join there is also a hard 'beak' so cut this out and discard it. Separate the tentacles and set aside. Pull the two 'wings' of the body and discard them as they can be quite chewy. Inside the squid tube there is a long thin piece of cartilage, pull it out and discard it. Scrape the darkish skin off the outside of the body then cut the body into 5 mm (¼ in)-wide rings.

Place both of the flours, corn maize and fine sea salt into a large bowl and stir to combine. Pour the oil in a pan or deep fryer and heat to 150°C/300°F. If you don't have a fryer drop a small piece of white bread in the oil; it should be golden brown after a couple of minutes. Lower the sliced garlic into the oil and fry until lightly browned and crisp, then transfer to kitchen towel to soak up any excess oil.

Repeat with the chilli, then heat the oil to 180°C/350°F. Add wet squid pieces to the flour mix and toss until each piece is coated. Fry in batches for 30–40 seconds, or until slightly golden and crisp. Transfer to paper towels to soak up any excess oil.

Place the squid on a serving dish then scatter the fried garlic and chilli over the top. Sprinkle salt and serve with the alioli for dipping on the side.

Crisp fried chicken marinated in almond and garlic

Oilasko frijitua almendra eta baratxuritan marinaturik

Pollo frito al ajillo y almendras

This creamy almond and garlic marinade works so well with chicken. Ideally you should marinate the chicken overnight to get the flavour through to the centre of the flesh.

After dredging in the dry mix, leaving the chicken to sit for 20 minutes or so allows any excess moisture to soak into the flour, making it extra crispy so don't skip this step. Finally, as with all frying, make sure your oil is clean and really hot or you will end up with a soggy coating.

I like to serve this simply with a few lemon wedges to squeeze over the top or a pot of *mojo rojo (see Basics)* for dipping.

Serves 4

4 garlic cloves, peeled

55 g (2 oz) flaked almonds

1 teaspoon sea salt

300 ml (10 fl oz) milk

4 boneless and skinless chicken thighs

50 g (1¾ oz) plain (all-purpose) flour

50 g (1¾ oz) cornflour (cornstarch)

100 g (3½ oz) self-raising (self-rising) flour

100 g (3½ oz) fine white maize flour
   (see pantry)

½ teaspoon sea salt

Vegetable oil, for frying, at least 1 litre
   (1¾ pints)

1 lemon, cut into wedges

First make the marinade. Place the garlic cloves, flaked almonds and salt in a pan with the milk then bring to a simmer. Remove from the heat and pour into a food processor. Purée till smooth then leave to cool.

Cut the chicken into 2.5 cm (1 in) strips then place in a glass or ceramic dish. Pour over the almond marinade then stir to evenly coat every strip. Cover and refrigerate for at least an hour (but ideally overnight) to marinate.

Mix the flours until well combined. Remove the chicken from the marinade and wipe off any excess liquid. Place each strip in the flour mixture and toss to coat. Remove the chicken from the flour and shake off any excess. Reserve the flour mixture for extra dusting. Place chicken strips in a single layer on a baking tray and set aside for at least 20 minutes.

Pour the vegetable oil into a pan or deep fryer and heat to 180°C/350°F. If you don't have a fryer use a sugar thermometer to check the temperature of the oil, or drop a small piece of white bread in the oil. The bread should turn golden brown after 30 seconds. While the oil is heating give the chicken another quick dusting in the dry mix then shake off any excess.

Once the oil is hot add half of the chicken and fry until golden and crisp. Remove one chicken strip and cut with a knife to check it is cooked through. If cooked, remove the remaining chicken strips from the oil and arrange them on paper towels to soak up any excess oil.

Repeat with the other half of the chicken, then serve on a platter with the lemon wedges.

Seared cod cheeks with caviar remoulade

Bakailao-kokotxa arrautzaztatuak kabiar maionesarekin

Kokotxas de bacalao rebozadas con mayonesa de caviar

This is a simple but elegant dish that makes use of the gelatinous and almost sweet cheek part of the cod, which is considered a delicacy in Spain, especially in the Basque region. The cheeks or *kokotxas*, are a lovely little nugget of flesh worth looking out for so if your fishmonger doesn't have them ask them to get him in for you. *Rebozadas* is a popular method of cooking in Spain where fish is dipped in flour then beaten egg, which results in a beautiful soft and slightly puffed coating. If you want a really crunchy crust, toss the cheeks in a bowl of panko breadcrumbs after the egg, before frying.

Seared cod cheeks with caviar remoulade

SERVES 4

50 ml (1¾ fl oz) milk
180 ml (6 fl oz) mayonnaise (see Basics)
50 g (1¾ oz) sevruga caviar
500 g (1¼ lb) cod cheeks (you can also use hake or monkfish cheeks)
50 g (1¾ oz) plain (all-purpose) flour
2 eggs
Olive oil, for frying
Coarse sea salt
Small bunch of chives, finely chopped
Bamboo skewers, optional

Whisk the milk into the mayonnaise until well combined then gently fold in the caviar. Cover and set aside.

Place the cheeks in a large bowl and pat dry with paper towels. Sprinkle over the flour, then toss to coat evenly and set aside.

In another bowl, beat the eggs till light and fluffy. Pour about 5 mm(¼ in) of olive oil in a frying pan and heat over medium-high heat. Working in batches of about six or seven shake the excess flour off the cod, then dip into the egg. Fry in the hot oil for 30 seconds on each side then transfer to paper towels, and keep warm while cooking the next batch. Repeat until all the cod cheeks are cooked and season with sea salt. Spread the caviar mixture on a plate, then arrange the cod cheeks on top and sprinkle with the chives, or alternatively, spike three cheeks onto bamboo skewers and serve upright 'pintxo style'.

Grilled octopus with oregano potatoes and smoked paprika

Olagarroa plantxan oregano-patata eta piperrauts ketuarekin

Pulpo a la plancha con patatas de orégano y pimentón ahumado

Every time I visit the Basque country I always go to a hole-in-the-wall pintxo bar called La Cuchara De San Telmo in the old part of San Sebastian. Despite being hard to find, it's always full. I always choose the grilled octopus, which the chef has mastered. It's slowly braised before being grilled until the edges are slightly charred, then served with a small mound of sautéed cabbage drizzled with olive oil. The grilling gives a wonderful smoky flavour and the almost crispy caramelised tentacles offer an interesting texture. This recipes is served with soft boiled potatoes and a sprinkling of smoked paprika, and I also add oregano for a touch of freshness.

Grilled octopus with oregano potatoes and smoked paprika

SERVES 4

1.2 kg (2½ lbs) octopus, rinsed in cold water
1 large brown onion, peeled and cut into quarters
1 large carrot, peeled and cut into large chunks
2 garlic cloves, peeled
1 bay leaf
400 g (14 oz) baby new potatoes
45 ml (3 tablespoons) extra virgin olive oil
15 ml (1 tablespoon) lemon juice
Small handful flat leaf parsley, finely chopped
1 tablespoon oregano or marjoram leaves, finely chopped
Mild olive oil, for grilling
Spanish sweet smoked paprika
Coarse sea salt

Bring a large pan (big enough to hold the octopus) of seasoned water to the boil.

Use a sharp knife to cut around the beak of the octopus, which is in the middle where the tentacles join up. Remove the beak then turn the head inside out, discarding the innards.

Rinse the octopus under cold running water then, tentacles first, slowly lower into the boiling water. Add the, onion, carrot, garlic and bay leaf, then bring the water back to a very gentle simmer. Cook for 45 minutes to 1 hour or until tender. The time can vary so check by piercing the thickest part of a tentacle with a skewer to see if it's tender. Once cooked, remove from the heat and leave the octopus to cool in its liquid.

Meanwhile, peel the potatoes then place in a pan and cover with cold water. Bring to a simmer and cook until tender then tip in a colander to drain. Once cool enough to handle, slice the potatoes into 1 cm (½ in) slices and place in a bowl. Place the olive oil, lemon juice, parsley and oregano or marjoram in a small bowl and whisk together. Pour the mixture over the potatoes along with a sprinkling of coarse sea salt. Toss the potatoes to coat them in mixture, then leave at room temperature to marinate.

Lift the octopus from the cooking liquid and drain in a colander. Discard the liquid and vegetables. Using a knife, remove the head and cut into a few large strips, then cut each tentacle on an angle into a few pieces. Toss with a little light olive oil to coat, and season with course sea salt.

Heat a grill pan or heavy frying pan over medium to high heat then sear the octopus segments until slightly charred and heated through. Arrange the potatoes on a flat serving dish and pour over any oil mixture, then arrange the octopus on top. Sprinkle with a little smoked paprika and coarse sea salt before serving.

Mussels in smoked paprika escabeche with bread crisps

Muskuiluak piperrauts ketu eskabetxean ogi kurruskariarekin

Mejillones en escabeche de pimentón ahumado con pan crujiente

As a kid I loved eating smoked mussels straight from a can with nothing more than plain biscuits or bread to soak up the smoky oil. On a recent trip to Spain while enjoying a plate of smoky chargrilled mussels my memories came flooding back . Later I was experimenting with different types of escabeche and tried seasoning some with smoked paprika. Straightaway I knew it would be perfect with mussels, the smoked paprika mimicking the flavour and the rich red oil on the escabeche took me back to my love of the canned variety.

Serves 4

80 ml (2¾ fl oz) olive oil
1 small carrot, cut into a matchsticks
1 small onion, peeled and finely sliced.
2 garlic cloves, peeled and finely sliced
Small pinch saffron
1 bay leaf
1 teaspoon sweet smoked paprika
6 white peppercorns
50 ml (1¾ fl oz) white wine vinegar
2 teaspoons caster (superfine) sugar
150 ml (5 fl oz) water
½ teaspoon coarse sea salt
1 kg (2¼ lb) mussels, de-bearded and rinsed in cold water
1 portion bread crisps or pan crujiente (see Basics)

Heat the olive oil in a small pan over medium heat then add the carrot, onion, garlic and saffron. Cook gently while stirring until slightly softened. Add the bay leaf, paprika, peppercorns, vinegar, sugar and water and bring to the boil. Add the salt, turn down the heat and simmer for 2 minutes. Remove from the heat and set aside.

Meanwhile, in a pan large enough to hold the mussels bring 250 ml (8½ fl oz) water to a boil over high heat. Add the mussels to the pan and cover. Cook for 2–3 minutes, shaking the pan every minute, until all the mussels have opened. Remove from the heat and pour the mussels into a colander. Once cool enough to handle pick the mussels from the shells, discarding any that have not opened, and put the mussel meat into a non-metallic dish.

Pour the cooled escabeche marinade and vegetables over the mussels then cover and refrigerate for at least 3 hours to marinate. Serve the mussels at room temperature with crisp bread.

Cockles cooked in white wine with cannellini beans, pancetta and torn croutons

Almejak babarrun txuri, hirugihar, eta ogi-mami kurruskariarekin

Almejas con alubias blancas, panceta y migas crujientes

Cockles and pancetta work so well together I could eat this wonderful combination every day. The sweetness of the cockles combined with the salty pancetta and a dash of chilli works so well together and the addition of cannellini beans adds a satisfying texture to the dish. For an unexpected contrast a sprinkling of crisp breadcrumbs or *migas* finishes it perfectly. Cockles, clams, palourde – technically they are not the same, but are so similar you can use any in this dish with exactly the same result. If your fishmonger has them, I recommend using English cockles. The combination of cockles and pancetta is quite salty so you shouldn't have to season the dish once cooked.

Cockles cooked in white wine with cannellini beans, pancetta and torn croutons

SERVES 4

30 ml (2 tablespoons) olive oil

100 g (3½ oz) stale white bread, torn into fingernail-sized pieces

25 g (¾ oz) smoked pancetta, chopped into thin strips (about 4 thin slices)

½ small onion, peeled and finely diced

½ small red chilli, finely chopped (remove the seeds
   if you don't want it too hot)

½ bay leaf

1 garlic clove, peeled and finely chopped

100 ml (3½ fl oz) dry white wine

50 ml (1½ fl oz) water

100 g (3½ oz) dry cannellini beans, cooked (see Pantry)
   or 1 x 400 g (14 oz) can of cooked cannellini beans, drained and rinsed

500 g (1¼ lb) cockles, purged (See Pantry)

Handful flat leaf parsley, finely chopped

Heat half the olive oil in a frying pan over medium-high heat. Add the bread to the pan and sauté until golden and crisp while shaking the pan, then transfer to some paper towels to absorb the excess oil.

Heat the remaining olive oil in pan large enough to hold the clams, then add the pancetta and gently sauté while stirring until it starts to brown and crisp. Add the onion, chilli, bay leaf and garlic, cooking while stirring till the onion is soft and translucent (about 5–6 minutes). Increase the heat and add the white wine and water. Bring to the boil and leave to bubble for a couple of minutes before adding the cannellini beans and cockles. Cover with a lid and cook, shaking every few moments until all the cockles have opened (about 4–5 minutes). Before serving, remove any cockles that haven't opened and discard them. Transfer to a serving dish then scatter the migas and parsley over the top.

Pancetta-wrapped new potatoes with sherry vinegar alioli and manchego

Hirugihar patatak jerez ozpin alliolia eta mantxego gaztarekin

Patatas envueltas en panceta con alioli de jerez y manchego

Crispy pancetta wrapped around soft potatoes makes perfect comfort food and the addition of shaved manchego with sherry vinegar alioli makes these potatoes wickedly moreish. For a lighter alternative, leave out the alioli and manchego then toss the potatoes through a bowl of mixed leaves dressed with sherry vinegar vinaigrette.

Pancetta-wrapped new potatoes with sherry vinegar alioli and manchego

SERVES 4

20 baby new potatoes (about 600 g/1 lb 5 oz)
20 thin slices of pancetta
Olive oil, for drizzling
100 ml (3½ fl oz) alioli (see Basics)
55 g (2oz) Manchego cheese
Small bunch of chives finely chopped

Put the potatoes in a small pan, cover with cold water and bring to a simmer. Cook for 10–15 minutes or until tender then tip into a colander to drain and cool.

Preheat the oven to 200°C/400°F/Gas mark 6.

Wrap each cold potato with a slice of pancetta and arrange on a baking tray lined with baking paper, with the loose end of the pancetta underneath (this will stop it from unwrapping while cooking). Drizzle with the olive oil then roast in the oven for about 10 minutes or until the pancetta is crisp on the edges. Meanwhile, make the sherry vinegar alioli. Once the potatoes are cooked, place in a serving dish then sprinkle over the shaved Manchego and chives. Serve with the alioli on the side or drizzle over the potatoes, if you prefer.

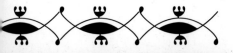

Mushrooms cooked with garlic and sherry on toast

Baratxuri eta jerez onddo brotxeta

Brocheta de setas al ajillo con jerez

Gutsy, meaty and satisfying, mushrooms on toast has always been a classic and this version takes it to the next level. Drenched in garlic and parsley then finished with a glazing of sherry, the flavour of the mushrooms are boosted while the pan-toasted bread soaks up the juices and adds a delightful crunch to each bite. You can use any dry to medium sweet sherry for this dish but I particularly like cooking with oloroso which adds a sweet richness.

Skewering the mushrooms really adds to the presentation but, of course, you could just spoon them over the toast if you prefer. The selection of mushrooms is up to you, but try to make sure they are the same size so they cook evenly.

Mushrooms cooked with garlic and sherry on toast

MAKES 8

2 large field mushrooms
150 g (5 oz) chestnut mushrooms
150 g (5 oz) oyster mushrooms
30 ml (2 tablespoons) aceite de ajo y perejil, (see Basics)
8 slices fresh baguette
Olive oil, for frying
50 ml (1½ fl oz) Oloroso sherry
Small handful flat leaf parsley, finely chopped
Extra virgin olive oil, for drizzling
Coarse sea salt

Peel the skin off each field mushroom and cut into eight wedges. Cut the chestnut mushrooms into two or three thick slices then tear the oyster mushrooms into similar-sized pieces. Thread the mushrooms onto the skewers in the following order: a wedge of field mushroom, a slice of oyster mushroom, a piece of chestnut mushroom, then oyster slice, field wedge, oyster slice and finish with a piece of chestnut mushroom. Skewering the mushrooms in this order helps them stay together when cooking. Repeat with all the skewers then brush on all sides with the *aceite de ajo y perejil*.

Coat a heavy frying pan with olive oil and heat. Toast the bread in the oil till golden and crisp on each side. Set aside and keep warm while cooking the mushrooms. Using the same pan, sauté the mushroom skewers on each side for 2 minutes until golden on the edges and cooked through. Add the sherry to the hot pan and as it bubbles and reduces roll the mushroom skewers in the sherry to glaze. Divide the skewers between the toasted bread then garnish each with a little chopped flat leaf parsley. Sprinkle over a little coarse sea salt and a drizzle of extra virgin olive oil before serving.

Salt cod brandade with tomato, almond and basil

Bakailao brandada tomate, almendra eta albakarekin

Brandada de bacalao con tomate, almendra, y albahaca

Brandada de bacalao is just one of the hundreds of common salt-cod preparations popular throughout Spain and neighbouring France. Every region has its own idea of how it should be prepared, what should go in it and with what it should be served. Most commonly it's a simple emulsion of salt cod, garlic and olive oil. It is commonly served simply as a winter dish with bread or potatoes.

My favourite version comes from the Basque Country where the potato is emulsified into the purée giving it a lighter, smoother texture and a milder flavour. For contrast I like to sprinkle the brandada with a mixture of chopped sun-blush tomatoes with almonds before serving. Be economical with the salt, as the bacalao is quite salty, even after soaking.

Salt cod brandade with tomato, almond and basil

SERVES 4

150 g (5 oz) floury potatoes, peeled and cut into even-sized chunks
300 ml (10 fl oz) milk
2 garlic cloves, peeled
1 bay leaf
300 g (10 oz) salt cod, desalinated (see Pantry)
150 ml (5 fl oz) mild olive oil
20 g (¾ oz) flaked almonds
50 g (1¾ oz) sun blush or semi-dried tomatoes in oil
Small handful basil leaves
Extra virgin olive oil, for drizzling

Place the potatoes in a pan and cover with cold water. Bring to a simmer and cook until tender, then drain in a colander.

Meanwhile in another small pan in which the salt cod fits snugly, heat the milk, garlic and bay leaf to a simmer. Add the salt cod and return to a simmer then cook for another minute or so until the cod just starts to flake. Remove from the heat and leave to steep for 5 minutes. Drain the milk from the cod and reserve 50 ml (1½ fl oz) along with the garlic. Discard the remaining milk and bay leaf.

In a bowl, flake the cod into small pieces, discarding the skin and any bones, then put in a food processor with the reserved milk and garlic. Pulse a few times to break up the cod then add the potato and pulse until smooth. With the motor still running drizzle in the olive oil to make an emulsion, then transfer to a serving dish. Season with salt, if needed.

Heat a dry frying pan over medium heat then add the almonds. Shake the pan while toasting the almonds until golden. Set aside to cool then roughly chop. Roughly chop the tomatoes and shred the basil then mix with the almonds. Scatter the mix over the top of the brandada then drizzle with a little extra virgin olive oil. Serve at room temperature with good bread or Bread Crisps (see Basics).

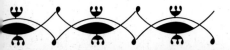

Tomato bread with salted smoked anchovies

Ogia tomate eta antxoa ketuekin

Pan con tomate y anchoas ahumadas

The cold water of the Cantabrian sea is home to some of the best anchovies in the world and many end up in the fishing villages on the Basque coast between Bilbao and San Sebastian. The anchovies are sized and auctioned off, to be eaten fresh or preserved by salt curing or pickling in vinegar. Basque anchovies are a premium product with an almost sweet meatiness.

At a recent anchovy tasting in Barcelona I was introduced to anchovies that had been smoked over birch wood before being cured. The flavour is outstanding and to really let them shine I simply serve them on the traditional *Catalan pan con tomate* which works so well with the smoky flesh. Smoked anchovies are available from good Spanish delicatessens but if you can't find them you can use any good Basque anchovy such as the beautifully packaged Ortiz brand.

MAKES 8

2 plum tomatoes
8 thick slices of crusty ciabatta
1 garlic clove, peeled
60 ml (4 tablespoons) extra virgin olive oil
8 smoked anchovy fillets in oil, drained
Coarse sea salt
Freshly ground black pepper

Bring a pan of water to the boil then add the tomatoes. Boil for 20 seconds or until the skins split then immediately plunge into them ice-cold water to cool for a few minutes. Drain the tomatoes and pat dry with a paper towel then roughly chop into a small dice. Toast the bread under a heated grill until golden and crisp. Rub each slice of the toasted bread with the garlic clove and drizzle with oil. Divide the chopped tomato over the top of each slice of bread. Place a smoked anchovy fillet on top of each then sprinkle with a little coarse sea salt and freshly ground black pepper.

Chorizo-spiced pork shoulder skewers

Moruno pintxoa

Pintxo moruno

Introduced to Spain by the Moors during their occupation *pintxo moruno* (Moorish skewer) was typically made with lamb until the majority of the population turned to Christianity, thus allowing them to eat pork. These days, they are made with any type of meat and every chef has his or her own spice blend to rub into the meat before grilling.

Pork shoulder is a really tasty cut of meat, with a bit of fat to keep it moist while cooking, it's perfect for grilling. I love chorizo so I like to flavour the pork with the same spices to really give it a flavour boost. The addition of sugar to the marinade adds a touch of sweetness but more importantly helps the meat develop a caramelised outside crust when cooking. Make sure to get a good bit of colour on the meat while grilling, as it really does add to the flavour.

Chorizo-spiced pork shoulder skewers

MAKES 8

1 garlic clove, peeled and ground
½ teaspoon coarse sea salt
1 teaspoon caster (superfine) sugar
2 teaspoons sweet smoked paprika
30 ml (2 tablespoons) olive oil, plus extra for cooking
400 g (14 oz) pork shoulder, diced into 2.5 cm (1 in) cubes
1 bay leaf, torn into small pieces
½ teaspoon ground cumin
8 slices of fresh baguette
150 ml (5 fl oz) piquillo pepper sauce (optional, see Basics)

In a glass or stainless-steel bowl combine the garlic, salt, sugar, paprika, cumin and olive oil and mix to a smooth paste. Dice the pork and add it to the paste with the bay leaf. Stir to coat each piece of meat evenly with the marinade. Cover and chill and leave to marinate for at least an hour (overnight is best).

Thread the pork onto skewers and discard any bits of bay leaf. You should have 3–4 pieces of meat for each skewer. Heat a little olive oil in grill pan or frying pan over high heat and, once smoking, grill the skewers for about 2 minutes on each side. Make sure they get some good colour, as this adds to the flavour.

Serve each skewer on a slice of baguette drizzled with a little olive oil and the piquillo pepper sauce.

Salt cod tartare with tomatoes, peppers, black olives and bread crisps

'Esqueixada' ogi kurruskariarekin

Esqueixada con pan crujiente

Light refreshing and full of the flavours of the Mediterranean, different versions of *esqueixada* are served all through Catalonia and its neighbouring regions. It's typically a rustic salad of raw salt cod, peppers and tomatoes simply dressed with olive oil and lemon juice. The name actually refers to the preparation of the cod, meaning to rip or tear it up. It really is a wonderful salad and I think it works really well diced then served like a tartare to be scooped up with bread crisps. Again, as with all bacalao recipes, be careful with the seasoning, as the cod will be quite salty, even after soaking.

Salt cod tartare with tomatoes, peppers, black olives and bread crisps

Serves 4

200 g (7 oz) salt cod loin, desalinated (see Basics)
60 ml (2 fl oz) extra virgin olive oil
½ small red onion, peeled and finely diced
½ green (bell) pepper (capsicum), deseeded, membrane removed and diced
2 plum tomatoes, de-seeded and diced
10 black olives, finely chopped
Small handful flat leaf parsley, finely shredded
15 ml (1 tablespoon) white wine vinegar
15 ml (1 tablespoon) lemon juice
Bread crisps, to serve (see Basics)

Finely dice the salt cod into pea-sized pieces then place in a bowl and cover with the olive oil. Place the diced onion in a bowl, cover with cold water and leave to soak for 10 minutes. Drain and pat dry with a paper towel. Add to the salt cod along with the diced pepper, tomatoes, olives and parsley. Pour over the lemon juice and white wine vinegar. Toss everything together until well combined then refrigerate for 20 minutes to allow the flavours to meld.

Divide the tartare between four plates, using a ring mould to shape it into neat circles. Drizzle over a little more olive oil, then serve with the bread crisps on the side.

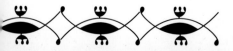

Prawn brochette with caramelised shallot salsa

Ganba brotxeta txalota karamelatu saltsarekin

Brocheta de gambas con salsa de chalota caramelizada

I recreated this recipe from a dish I ate on my first visit to the Basque Country. Bar Goiz Argi in the old part of San Sebastian serves a selection of stunning pintxos and the *brocheta de gambas* are the most popular. Every night of the week the tiny bar fills with locals standing shoulder to shoulder with a glass of the local wine *txakoli* in one hand and a *brocheta de gambas* in the other. With such a simple pintxo it's important to get the best quality prawns you can and not to overcook them as they will toughen if left in the pan for a second too long.

Prawn brochette with caramelised shallot salsa

MAKES 8

Olive oil, for frying, plus 75 ml (5 tablespoons) extra virgin olive oil
4 small round shallots, peeled and finely chopped
5 cm (2 in) length of carrot, finely diced
30 ml (2 tablespoons) white wine vinegar
1 teaspoon caster (superfine) sugar
½ red (bell) pepper (capsicum), seeded and finely chopped
Coarse sea salt
24 raw king prawns, shelled and de-veined
8 slices of fresh baguette
Small bunch of chives, finely chopped

Heat 1 tablespoon of the olive oil in a small pan over low heat. Add the shallot and carrot and cook gently while stirring, every couple of minutes, until soft and sweet, about 15 minutes. Stir in the vinegar and sugar then continue to cook for another couple of minutes until the vinegar has evaporated. Remove from the heat then stir in the red pepper, remaining olive oil and coarse sea salt to taste.

Thread three prawns on each skewer side by side. Heat a small glug of olive oil in a frying pan over medium-high heat. Add the prawn skewers and cook for 1 minute, turn, and cook for another 30 seconds or until the prawns are just opaque in the middle.

Place a skewer on each slice of bread then divide the salsa between each before sprinkling with chopped chives.

Sweet spiced lamb ribs with sweet potato purée

Arkume-sahaski gozoak batata purearekin

Costillas de cordero dulces con puré de batata

Cheaper cuts of meat, especially those still on the bone, are perfect for this type of preparation. Slowly braised in sweet spices until meltingly tender then sautéed to crisp the skin, these lamb ribs are so moreish you'll wish you had made more. I've tried many lamb dishes in bars across the Basque Country where the chefs are really pushing the limits with their cooking and once had a dish similar to this in a pintxo bar in Bilbao. I can't quite remember the name of the bar, but I can definitely remember how good the ribs tasted, and I just had to give it a go myself.

Sweet spiced lamb ribs with sweet potato purée

SERVES 4

1 teaspoon cumin seeds
½ teaspoon ground cinnamon
15 ml (1 tablespoon) olive oil
2 garlic cloves, peeled and ground with 1 teaspoon coarse sea salt
30 ml (2 tablespoons) honey
800 g (1¾ lb) lamb ribs
300 ml (10 fl oz) chicken stock
100 ml (3½ fl oz) pedro ximinex sherry
Olive oil, for frying
Small handful of flat leaf parsley, finely shredded

SWEET POTATO PURÉE

600 g (1 lb 5 oz) sweet potato, peeled and cut into even sized chunks
30 ml (2 tablespoons) extra virgin olive oil
Coarse sea salt

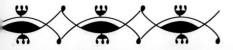

Toast the cumin seeds in a dry pan over medium high heat for about 20 seconds or until aromatic, then grind to a powder with a mortar and pestle. In a bowl, place the cumin, cinnamon, olive oil, garlic and honey and whisk to a paste. Pour the paste over the ribs and massage into the meat then cover and refrigerate for at least an hour to marinate.

Cut the ribs into groups of three ribs joined together and put in a large bowl.

Preheat the oven to 150°C/300°F/Gas mark 2.

Place the ribs and marinade in a small, high-edged baking tray and pour in the chicken stock and sherry. Cover tightly with aluminium foil and bake for 2 hours.

Meanwhile, place the sweet potato in a pan and cover with cold water. Bring to the boil then reduce the heat to a simmer and cook for 15 minutes or until tender. Drain the sweet potato in a colander and once dry, return to a clean pan and place over a low heat. Stir for a few minutes to steam dry then add the olive oil and season with salt. Mash with the back of a fork or potato masher and set aside to re-heat when serving.

Drain the cooked ribs in a colander, retaining the liquid. Pass the liquid through a fine sieve into a small pan then skim off and discard the fat. Place over a medium heat until reduced by half.

Coat a non-stick frying pan with olive oil. Heat, and add the ribs skin side down. Sauté till crisp on the edges. Turn the ribs and continue cooking. When heated through, transfer the ribs to a bowl. Pour the reduced cooking liquid over the ribs and toss to coat. Spoon sweet potato purée onto a serving platter and place the ribs on top. Garnish with a sprinkling of shredded parsley.

Red mullet in fennel escabeche with lemon-scented lentils

Barbarinak mihilu-eskabetxean limoi lentejekin

Salmonetes en escabeche de hinojo con lentejas al limón

Marinating in escabeche was traditionally a method of preservation used before refrigeration and is now a common technique used to impart a flavour into fish and poultry dishes in Spain. The acid in the vinegar preserves the flesh while the aromatic ingredients give flavour and add texture. Typically escabeche is quite an acidic dish so without the need for vinegar as a method of preservation I have knocked the vinegar content back to a minimum. The addition of a little honey provides sweetness that balances the acidity, and the fennel is the perfect flavour match to red mullet. I find that most oily fish, such as mackerel, salmon and sardines, work well in this recipe.

Red mullet in fennel escabeche with lemon-scented lentils

SERVES 4

80 ml (2¾ fl oz) mild olive oil, plus extra
for frying
3 baby fennel finely sliced, save the fronds
to garnish the dish
1 small carrot, peeled and sliced into thin
rounds
1 shallot, peeled and finely sliced.
1 garlic clove, peeled and
finely sliced
1 bay leaf
½ tsp sweet paprika
5 white peppercorns
50 ml (1½ fl oz) sherry vinegar
Small pinch saffron
15 ml (1 tablespoon) honey
150 ml (5 fl oz) water
Coarse sea salt
4 red mullet fillets (about 50 g/1¾ oz each)
pin boned and scaled

LENTILS

100 g (3½ oz) Puy or small
green lentils
Peel from ½ lemon, white
pith removed
Good handful flat leaf parsley,
finely chopped
15 ml (1 tablespoon) extra-virgin olive oil
Zest from half a lemon
Salt
Small handful baby fennel cress

Prepare the lentils. Put the lentils and lemon peel in a pan and cover with water. Bring to a simmer for 20–25 minutes or until tender. Once cooked, drain the lentils into a colander and allow to cool. Discard the peel.

Meanwhile, to make the escabeche heat the olive oil in a small pan over medium heat, and add the fennel, carrot, shallot and garlic. Cook gently while stirring until the onion and carrots start to soften. Add the bay leaf, paprika, peppercorns, vinegar, saffron, honey and water then bring to the boil. Turn down to a gentle simmer and season with a sprinkling of coarse sea salt.

Heat a small glug of olive oil in a non-stick pan over a medium–high heat. Season the red mullet fillets, then fry skin side down until cooked halfway through. Remove the fillets from the pan and arrange in a single layer, skin side up, in a glass or ceramic dish. Pour the hot escabeche marinade over the fish and leave at room temperature to cool. The residual heat will finish cooking the fish.

Mix the cooked lentils with the chopped parsley, olive oil, lemon zest and a sprinkling of salt and spoon onto a flat serving dish. Spoon over the escabeche vegetables and some of the juices, then arrange the red mullet fillets on top. Serve at room temperature garnished with the reserved fennel fronds.

Salmon ceviche with palm heart, fennel and apple

Izozkin zebitxea a palmondo bihotza, mihilu eta sagarrarekin

Ceviche de salmón con corazón de palmito, hinojo y manzana

South America immigrants living in Spain brought with them new dishes and techniques such as Peru's national dish ceviche. Dressed with citrus, the acid in the juice 'cooks' the proteins in the fish without using any heat.

I first tried ceviche while holidaying in Mexico and was surprised by its clarity in flavour. It wasn't at all 'fishy' and was so refreshing in the Mexican heat. Since then I've made many ceviche preparations and this is one of my favourites. Salmon and fennel work well together and the addition of palm hearts adds a creamy texture. The apple adds crunch along with sweetness.

Make sure you buy the freshest salmon you can and cut it thinly. Canned palm hearts can be found in Spanish and Caribbean delicatessens and good supermarkets.

Salmon ceviche with palm heart, fennel and apple

SERVES 4

½ teaspoon salt

1 teaspoon sugar

45 ml (3 tablespoons) lemon juice

45 ml (3 tablespoons) extra virgin olive oil

3 spring onions, finely sliced

300 g (10 oz) salmon, skinned and pin-boned

½ Granny Smith apple

6 baby fennel, outer layer removed and very finely shaved

3 x 7.5 cm (3in) lengths of palm hearts in brine, drained and sliced
    into 5 mm (¼ in) thick slices

Extra virgin olive oil, to finish

Coarse sea salt, to finish

Small handful of coriander (cilantro), finely chopped

In a large bowl, whisk the salt and sugar with the lemon juice until dissolved. Whisk in the olive oil then stir in the sliced spring onion. Cut the salmon lengthways down the middle, then slice into 5 mm (¼ in) thick slices.

Thirty minutes before serving, toss the salmon in the dressing until well coated. Cover the bowl with cling film (plastic wrap) and refrigerate to 'cook'.

Meanwhile, peel and core the apple and, using a peeler, shave it into thin pieces. Put in the mixing bowl with the salmon, spring onion, fennel and palm heart. Gently toss everything together and then spoon onto a flat serving dish. Drizzle with extra virgin olive oil and sprinkle over a little coarse sea salt and the coriander.

Spinach with chickpeas and pancetta

Espinakak txitxirio eta hirugiharrarekin

Espinacas con garbanzos y panceta

Popular in tapa bars all over Spain *espinacas con garbanzos* is another example of the Moors influence on Spanish cuisine. The same combination of ingredients is quite often used in soups and stews but this dryer version with the addition of pancetta is my favourite. The pancetta adds flavour and makes the dish more substantial but you can leave it out if you want. Great as a tapa, espinacas con garbanzos y panceta makes a delicious side dish to go with roast chicken or fish. Spanish pancetta is pretty much the same as the Italian equivalent so its fine to use either or try a good dry-cured bacon.

Spinach with chickpeas and pancetta

SERVES 4

30 ml (2 tablespoons) olive oil
80 g (2¾ oz) cured pancetta cut into lardons
1 garlic clove, peeled and finely sliced
½ small onion, finely chopped
250 g (9 oz) cooked chickpeas or 1 x 400 g (14 oz) can chickpeas,
*   rinsed and drained*
150 ml (5 fl oz) vegetable or chicken stock
200g (7oz) baby spinach, washed and drained
Salt

Using a large pan or frying pan, heat 30 ml (1 tablespoon) of olive oil over medium heat then add the pancetta lardons. Sauté until the fat is rendered out and the lardons are golden brown and crisp. Tip the lardons into a sieve and drain off the fat.

Return the pan to the heat then add the remaining olive oil. Add the garlic and onion and sauté for a couple of minutes until soft and translucent. Add the chickpeas and the stock and bring to a simmer. Reduce the stock by half then add the spinach and cooked lardons. Continue cooking for another couple of minutes while stirring until the spinach is wilted. Transfer to a serving dish and drizzle with a little olive oil. Serve hot.

Pork ribs slow roast in membrillo and sherry vinegar

Txerri-saiheskiak jerez ozpin eta irasagarrarekin erreta

Costillas de cerdo asadas con vinagre de jerez y membrillo

These slow-cooked pork ribs in a sticky marinade of honey and fruity quince paste are to die for. The vinegar adds a little bite similar to Chinese sweet and sour, which works so well with pork ribs.

The ribs really do benefit from marinating overnight to get the flavour right to the bone but even after just a few hours they will still taste fabulous. The constant basting while roasting ensures the ribs have a lovely glazed finish and also stops them from drying out.

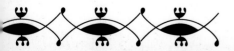

Pork ribs slow roast in membrillo and sherry vinegar

SERVES 4

100 g (3½ oz) quince paste (membrillo)
45 ml (3 tablespoons) honey
45 ml (3 tablespoons) sherry vinegar
2 garlic cloves, peeled
1 teaspoon hot paprika
800 g (1½ lb) pork ribs, separated
1 teaspoon coarse sea salt, plus extra for serving
Leaves from 3 sprigs rosemary
45 ml (3 tablespoons) olive oil

In a food processor combine the quince paste, honey, sherry vinegar, garlic and hot paprika then process to a smooth paste. Put the pork ribs in a deep tray, sprinkle over the salt and rosemary then pour over the marinade. Massage everything into the ribs then cover and refrigerate for at least 3 hours to marinate (if you can, marinate overnight for the best results).

Preheat the oven to 160°C/325°F/Gas mark 3.

Spread the ribs out on a roasting tray and drizzle over the olive oil. Place in the oven and roast for 1 hour 15 minutes basting with the pan juices every 15 minutes.

Turn the heat up to 200°C/400°F/Gas mark 6 and roast the ribs for another 15 minutes. At this stage of cooking keep an eye on the ribs as they will colour quite quickly. Baste the ribs with their own juices, turn and roast for another 15 minutes or until well coloured. Sprinkle with a little extra coarse sea salt.

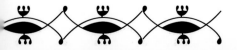

Talo with chistorra and piquillo pepper ketchup

Txistorra taloa pikillo ketchuparekin

Talo con chistorra y ketchup de piquillo

Talo is the Basque version of a soft corn tortilla similar to those found in Mexico. Most commonly eaten at markets and fiestas such as el día de Santo Tomás (Saint Thomas day) on the 21st December. Both the Basque cities of San Sebastian and Bilbao celebrate the day (and night) with a street market revolving around the beloved local sausage called *chistorra*, similar to chorizo but much thinner. Grilled chistorra is sold from market stalls wrapped in bread or talo then washed down with copious amounts of dry Basque cider.

A cross between a taco and a hotdog, *talo con chistorra* benefits from a sauce or salsa, so I smother them with piquillo pepper sauce.

You can buy chistorra from Spanish delicatessens, or use small chorizo sausages split down the middle lengthways before grilling

Talo with chistorra and piquillo pepper ketchup

MAKES 12

100 g (3½ oz) fine yellow corn maize (see Pantry)
¼ teaspoon salt
150 ml (5 fl oz) warm water
350 g (12 oz) chistorra sausage
Olive oil, for frying
150 ml (5 fl oz) piquillo pepper sauce (see Pantry)
Olive oil, for frying

Put the yellow corn maize and salt in a bowl and pour over the warm water. Stir to combine, then tip onto a clean work surface. Use your hands to knead the dough for 3–4 minutes to bring it together. Wrap the dough in cling film (plastic wrap) and refrigerate for 20 minutes. Meanwhile, cut the chistorra into 8 cm (3 in) lengths (the talo will shrink to this size when cooked).

Divide the dough into 12 balls and, using a rolling pin, flatten them into 8 cm (3 in) discs about 3 mm (⅛ in) thick onto a sheet of baking paper.

Coat a frying pan with olive oil and heat over medium heat. Fry each talo for 3 minutes on each side or until golden, adding a little oil after cooking every couple of talo to stop the pan becoming dry. Transfer the cooked talo to a plate and cover with foil and keep warm in a low oven.

Heat a small amount of oil in the same pan and add the lengths of chistorra, searing while turning until cooked through. Alternatively, if you prefer, you can simmer the chistorra in water for 4 minutes. Place a length of cooked chistorra on top of each talo then spoon some sauce over the top. Wrap the talo around then serve with a cold cider or beer.

EGGS

Arrautzak

HUEVOS

Sᴄʀᴀᴍʙʟᴇᴅ, ꜱᴛɪʀʀᴇᴅ ɪɴᴛᴏ ᴀ ꜱᴏᴜᴩ, ɪɴ ᴅᴇꜱꜱᴇʀᴛꜱ ᴏʀ ɪɴᴄᴏʀᴩᴏʀᴀᴛᴇᴅ into an omelette, eggs are an important ingredient in the cuisine of Spain. The Spanish use eggs in a huge variety of dishes, but without a doubt the Spanish omelette is the most popular.

Just about every bar in Spain will sell a classic *tortilla de patata* of some kind and perhaps a few other variations of Spain's best-known dish. Along the Basque coast *tortilla de bacalao*, a rich salt-cod omelette strewn with onion and green pepper, is one of the most popular alternatives, closely followed by smaller tortillas containing diced chorizo or jamón, usually served for breakfast wrapped in a small bread roll.

Huevos revueltos (eggs scrambled with mushrooms or seafood) is another popular dish, usually eaten as a first course to a meal at lunch or dinner time. During the wild mushroom season in the north of Spain *huevos revueltos con hongos* (scrambled eggs with mushrooms) will feature on most menus. When mushroom season finishes, they are replaced with salt cod or prawns.

Baked egg piperade with salted anchovies

Arrautz eta antxoa piperrada

Piperrada con huevo y anchoa

Rustic, homely and absolutely beautiful, *piperrada* baked with eggs is most common
in the French side of the Basque region but it's not unusual to see it on menus all over
Spain. Whenever I make piperade at home I always make sure I have enough to prepare
this simple dish the next day for a lazy brunch or light dinner.

On a recent trip to Catalonia I enjoyed a wonderful breakfast of fried eggs topped
with salted anchovies, which made me think of how great it would be with a mound of
piperade to cut into the saltiness. The combination of sweet piperade, salty anchovy and
creamy egg works perfectly together.

Baked egg piperade with salted anchovies

MAKES 4 TAPA SIZED PORTIONS

250g (8oz) of piperade (see Vegetables)
4 eggs
50 g (1 ¾ oz) salted anchovy fillets in oil, drained
Olive oil, for drizzling
Crusty bread, for serving

Preheat your oven to 200°C/400°F/Gas mark 6.

Divide the piperade between four small ceramic dishes, or *cazuelas*, then make a well in the centre for the egg. Crack an egg into each well and place a couple of anchovy fillets on top.

Drizzle each with a little olive oil and bake for 10 minutes or until the egg is just set. Leave to rest for a few minutes, then serve with crusty bread or toast.

Remember to warn everyone that the cazuelas are roasting hot!

Poached egg with chorizo, torn bread and peas

Ur erakinetan egindako arrautzak txorizo, ogi-mami eta ilarrekin

Huevos escalfados con chorizo, migas y guisantes

No one can deny how much chorizo and eggs go so well together and in this preparation the match is taken to a new level. Bread cooked in the chorizo oil or *migas* are a common dish served throughout the regions of Extremadura, Andalucía and La Mancha, and even though each region has their own recipes most are prepared in the same way – stale bread fried in animal fat. Many versions contain a mixture of sausages like chorizo and morcilla, or both, mixed with cheaper cuts of pork and sometimes lamb or goat. This simpler version is made with just chorizo but you can add any meat you like. Fatty meats such as bacon work well, giving off enough fat to fry the bread in. Peas aren't a usual addition but I think they add a freshness to the dish and the colour really adds to the presentation.

Poached egg with chorizo, torn bread and peas

MAKES 4 TAPA SIZED PORTIONS

100 g (3½ oz) frozen peas
30 ml (2 tablespoons) white wine vinegar (optional, but will help
  set the egg whites)
15 ml (1 tablespoon) olive oil
100 g (3½ oz) cooking chorizo, skinned and crumbled into small pieces
4 thick slices ciabatta, crust removed and torn into small pieces
4 eggs
Small handful pea shoots (optional)
Coarse sea salt

Bring a small pan of water to the boil and blanch the peas for a couple of minutes. Drain and plunge the peas into iced water to cool. Once chilled, drain the peas again and pat dry with paper towel.

Bring another pan of water to the boil and add the vinegar. Reduce the heat to a simmer.

Meanwhile, in a small frying pan, heat the olive oil over a medium heat. Add the chorizo and sauté for a few moments until it starts to release its oil and is cooked through. Spoon the chorizo from the pan, leaving the oil, and set aside. Return the pan to the heat and add the bread to the chorizo oil and sauté until crisp. Add the chorizo back to the pan along with the peas and keep cooking while tossing the pan, to heat through. Remove from the heat and keep warm.

Crack the eggs carefully into the simmering water and poach until the whites are set but the yolk is left runny. Use a slotted spoon to remove the eggs from the water and place in a colander to drain. Divide the chorizo, migas and peas between four small dishes and place a poached egg on top of each. Garnish with the pea shoots and sprinkle with a little coarse sea salt.

Potato and onion omelette

Patata tortilla tipularekin

Tortilla de patata con cebolla

Tortilla de patata is probably the most iconic dish to come out of Spain. For a dish that seems so simple it has quite a long method but each step is important. I like to use a floury variety of potato and cook it till it's almost like mash. Once the eggs are added, resting the mixture for a while before cooking enables the potato to soak up some of the egg, which helps with the texture.

While cooking it's important to watch the heat and you will probably need to keep turning it down. The idea is to cook it through before it becomes too dark on the outside. Personally, I like my tortilla quite moist in the middle, almost raw but it's up to you how long you cook it for, just watch the colour and be careful not to burn it. Finally, once it's cooked and turned out onto a plate, cover it tightly with cling film (plastic wrap) and leave it to rest. This allows the residual heat to finish cooking the tortilla and it also stops a dry skin forming on the surface.

Potato and onion omelette

MAKES A 25 CM (10 IN) TORTILLA

600 ml (1 pint) olive oil
800 g (1½ lb) floury potatoes, peeled, cut lengthways into quarters and
    sliced 3 mm (⅛ in) thick
½ small onion, peeled and finely diced
2 teaspoons coarse sea salt
6 eggs

In a 25 cm (10 in) frying pan heat the olive oil over medium heat and add the potato, onion and salt. Reduce the heat to a gentle simmer. The oil should only just be bubbling, if it's bubbling a lot turn the heat down. Gently cook, stirring every couple of minutes until the potatoes are starting to fall apart and crush easily when squashed with a fork. The idea is to not get any colour on the potatoes but to slowly confit without colouring, which takes about 20 minutes.

Drain the mixture into a colander or sieve over a bowl to catch the excess oil and leave for 5 minutes. Reserve the oil for cooking the tortilla. Transfer the potatoes to a large mixing bowl and, using a fork, break up and crush the potato mix till it's almost mushy. Set the mixture aside to cool to room temperature. When cool, break the eggs over the top. Whisk the mixture quickly just to break up the eggs and evenly distribute the potato mixture and leave for 30 minutes to soak.

Wipe the frying pan clean and return to a medium heat, adding enough of the reserved olive oil to cover the base of the pan. Once the oil is hot add the tortilla mixture and, using a rubber spatula, give it a quick stir while shaking the pan, then reduce the heat to low.

Gently cook the tortilla, shaking the pan every few minutes until the base is golden. Be careful not to burn it at this stage. (You can slide the spatula underneath and gently lift to see if the tortilla is cooking too quickly.) It will still be quite wet in the middle but don't worry about that at this stage.

Now the hard bit! To flip the tortilla, place a plate or even better a large pan lid over the frying pan and remove from the heat. Whatever you use make sure it has no lip or it will be really difficult to slide the tortilla back into the pan. Use one quick smooth motion and while firmly holding the plate or lid, flip the pan over. If all goes well the tortilla will now be sitting upside down and still be in one piece. Place the frying pan back on the heat and add enough of the reserved olive oil to cover the base of the pan again. Once hot, gently slide the tortilla back into the pan and continue cooking till it's golden.

Now using the same technique, flip the tortilla back onto a serving plate. Cover the hot tortilla with cling film (plastic wrap) making sure its directly touching the surface of the tortilla and leave for 10 minutes to rest before serving.

Fried eggs with chorizo-braised lentils

Lentejak txorizo eta arrautz frijituekin

Lentejas guisadas con chorizo y huevos fritos

This is such a comforting dish, perfect for brunch or for breakfast to heal the soul after a night of over-indulgence. Eggs and lentils work fantastically together, especially on a textural level when the soft yolk oozes over the top, almost creating another sauce. Lentils are great at absorbing flavours. I sometimes cook this dish with pancetta instead of chorizo, and quite often poach the eggs instead of frying them, but that's really up to you.

SERVES 4

60 ml (4 tablespoons) olive oil
200 g (7 oz) cooking chorizo, cut into thick slices
2 garlic cloves, peeled and finely chopped
1 medium onion, peeled and finely diced
1 medium carrot, peeled and finely diced
1 bay leaf
4 plum tomatoes, de-seeded and diced
200 g (7oz) small green Puy or brown lentils
1 litre (1¾ pints) water
4 eggs
Small handful of flat leaf parsley, finely shredded
Coarse sea salt
Extra virgin olive oil, to drizzle

Heat half the olive oil in a pan over medium heat. Add the chorizo and sauté until it releases its fat and is a light golden colour on each side. Remove the chorizo and set aside, leaving the oil in the pan. Add the garlic, onion and carrot and sweat down until soft. Add the bay leaf and tomatoes and continue cooking for a couple of minutes until the tomato turns pulpy.

Stir the lentils into the vegetables and add the water with a sprinkling of salt and bring to the boil. Reduce the heat to a gentle simmer and cook for 15–20 minutes or until the lentils are soft but not falling apart. Check the seasoning and add more salt if needed. Stir in the reserved chorizo and cook for another 3 minutes until cooked through.

Heat the remaining olive oil in a non-stick frying pan over a low–medium heat. Fry the eggs, sprinkle with a little coarse sea salt and remove from the heat.

Divide the lentils between 4 warm bowls and, using a slotted spoon, place the eggs on top. Sprinkle with the chopped parsley and a drizzle of extra virgin olive oil.

Scrambled eggs with prawn, green pepper and onion

Ganba eta piper-berde nahaskia

Revuelto de gambas y pimiento verde

The Spanish love eggs and will eat them any time of the day in dishes such as this, usually served as the first of a multi-course meal. In Spain, *huevos revueltos*, or more simply scrambled eggs, will often include seafood of some kind, commonly prawns or salt cod, and is not usually eaten for breakfast. In the Basque Country wild mushrooms are also another common ingredient, especially during autumn when the foraging season is in full swing. Whatever the addition, it's important that the eggs aren't overcooked or they will become watery and make the dish unpleasant. If you use frozen prawns, pat them dry thoroughly with a paper towel before adding to the eggs.

Makes 4 tapa sized portions

6 eggs

15 ml (1 tablespoon) light olive oil

½ small onion, peeled and finely diced

1 garlic clove, crushed with the flat edge of a knife blade

½ green bell pepper (capsicum), de-seeded and finely diced

1 red bell pepper (capsicum), de-seeded and finely diced

100 g (3½ oz) small prawns cooked and shelled

Small handful flat leaf parsley, finely chopped

Crusty bread or toast, to serve

Crack the eggs into a bowl and lightly whisk them. Set aside. Heat the olive oil in a pan over medium heat and add the onion and garlic. Cook gently while stirring for about 7–8 minutes until slightly golden and soft. Add the diced peppers and continue cooking for another 4–5 minutes or until the peppers are soft. Pour the eggs into the pan and using a wooden spoon continuously stir while scraping the cooked egg off the bottom of the pan. After the eggs look about half cooked add the prawns to the pan and continue cooking while stirring, until the eggs are nearly scrambled to your liking. The eggs will keep cooking a bit once you take them off the heat so don't overcook.

Scatter over the chopped parsley and serve straightaway with crusty bread or toast on the side.

Salt cod omelette

Bakailao tortilla

Tortilla de bacalao

Salt cod has found its way into just about every dish possible in Spain but one of my favourites – and also one of the simplest – is a salt cod omelette or *tortilla de bacalao*. Along with a traditional *tortilla de patata* most pintxo bars throughout the Basque Country will also have a salt cod omelette on offer, often being more popular than the potato version. Like all traditional dishes there are loads of versions of tortilla de bacalao, some containing potato or leek and lots of garlic. This version is more basic and has no potato, making it really quick to cook with just the addition of onion and green pepper for sweetness and parsley for added freshness. I have also made this omelette successfully with smoked haddock but I'm not too sure how well that would go down in the Basque Country!

Salt cod omelette

MAKES AN 20 CM (8 IN) TORTILLA

350 g (12 oz) salt cod loin, desalinated (see Basics)
1 litre (1¾ pints) boiling water
60 ml (4 tablespoons) olive oil
1 small onion, finely diced
1 green bell pepper (capsicum), finely diced
6 eggs, lightly beaten
Small handful flat leaf parsley, finely chopped

Put the salt cod in a sturdy bowl or pan and pour on the boiling water. Leave in the water for 5 minutes, then remove and drain. Pat dry with a paper towel and flake into small pieces, discarding the skin and any bones.

Heat 30 ml (2 tablespoons) of the olive oil in a 20cm (8 in) non-stick frying pan over a medium–low heat. Add the onion and sweat down until soft without colouring, about 5 minutes. Add the green pepper and continue cooking for another 5 minutes until soft. Remove from the heat and leave to cool for 5 minutes.

Stir the onion and pepper mixture into the beaten eggs along with the flaked salt cod and parsley. Wipe the pan clean and add another 30 ml (2 tablespoons) of olive oil and heat over a medium–low heat. Add all the egg mixture to the pan while gently shaking in a circular motion over the heat until the egg sets and releases itself from the surface of the pan. Turn the heat down to low and leave to cook for about 5 minutes or until about 50 per cent cooked through.

Check to make sure the surface of the egg isn't getting too dark, it should only have a slight golden tinge.

For the next step you really have to commit! Lightly oil a rimless plate and place upside down over the omelette. Hold onto the plate with one hand and the frying pan with the other then in one quick motion flip the pan over so that the tortilla is upside down on the plate.

Place the frying pan back on the heat and add the remaining olive oil.

Gently slide the tortilla back into the pan then use a spatula to push the edges of the egg towards the centre of the pan so you get a neat edge. Cook the tortilla for a couple of minutes or until cooked through. Test by pressing the centre of the tortilla, it should feel quite firm but make sure not to overcook it or the texture will become rubbery. Turn the tortilla out onto a plate and cover tightly with cling film (plastic wrap), making sure it's stuck to the surface of the tortilla to prevent a dry skin forming. Leave for at least 10 minutes before serving.

VEGETABLES

Barazkiak

VERDURAS

ON THE SURFACE, THE FOOD OF SPAIN and the Basque Country seems to be heavy with meat, pulses and seafood, but dig a little deeper and you'll see the importance of vegetables in many dishes. The Spanish diet is local and seasonal, and many households grow their own produce or shop from local greengrocers who only sell seasonal items.

Traditionally, the Spanish like their vegetables cooked until well done, and often until they can be squashed with the back of a fork. However, it's becoming popular for vegetables to be cooked briefly, preserving the colour and nutrients. Some dishes though do require the vegetables to be cooked a little more as in *ensaladilla rusa* where the texture should be soft, almost smooth and creamy.

The Spanish are masters of preservation and many households still preserve their own home-grown produce. These preserved vegetables are eaten simply with basic dressings while many, such as artichokes and asparagus, can be cooked with other seasonal vegetables in dishes such as *menestra de verduras* (vegetable stew).

Basque onion, pepper and tomato stew

Piperrada

Piperrada

When I think of Basque food the first thing to come to mind is the robust, gutsy flavours of *piperrada*. From the French Basque region, piperrada is a simple stew of onions, peppers and tomatoes cooked slowly together. It makes a good base for other dishes, or can be served on its own. During my time on Professional MasterChef I even used it as a sauce base by puréeing it with fish stock and serving it with monkfish. In this recipe I replaced the more traditional green peppers with yellow simply for the colour and added sweetness.

Basque onion, pepper and tomato stew

MAKES 250 G (9 OZ)

45 ml (3 tablespoons) olive oil
2 garlic cloves, peeled and finely sliced
1 large onion, peeled and finely into 2 cm (¾ in) pieces
1 bay leaf
1 red bell pepper (capsicum), de-seeded and sliced into 2 cm (¾ in) pieces
1 yellow bell pepper (capsicum), de-seeded and sliced into 2 cm (¾ in) pieces
3 plum tomatoes, de-seeded and roughly chopped, or
*   1 x 400 g (14 oz) can peeled, chopped tomatoes*
100 ml (3½ fl oz) water
Coarse sea salt

Heat the olive oil in a pan over medium heat. Add the garlic and gently sauté until slightly golden and aromatic.

Add the onion and bay leaf to the pan and sweat down, stirring occasionally until the onion is soft and translucent, about 5 minutes. Add the peppers to the pan and continue cooking, stirring every few minutes until softened, about 10 minutes.

Stir the tomato through the onion and pepper mix, add the water and reduce the heat to a low simmer. (If you are using a can of tomatoes omit the water.)

Very gently cook the piperrada for another 45 minutes to an hour, stirring frequently so it doesn't stick to the pan.

The piperrada is ready once most of the liquid has evaporated and it has a jam-like consistency. Season to taste, cool to room temperature and refrigerate. If you want to serve the piperrada as a side dish re-heat it in a small pan over a low heat.

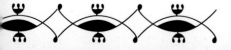

Cabbage and potato cakes

Trinxat

Trinxat

Trinxat, a Catalan preparation of potato and cabbage is not too different to champ potatoes, and is traditionally served with salted pork, but it goes well with just about anything. I love it with roast poultry or for a filling Sunday brunch, or try it with fried eggs, smoked bacon and morcilla. Trinxat can be served wet like mashed potatoes or more commonly formed into patties and fried, which gives it a lovely crisp golden crust.

Makes 8 patties

1 kg (2¼ lb) floury potatoes, peeled and cut into even chunks
45 ml (3 tablespoons) olive oil, plus extra for frying
2 garlic cloves, peeled and finely chopped
1 savoy cabbage, outer leaves removed and finely sliced
100 ml (3½ fl oz) water
Coarse sea salt
50 g (1¾ oz) plain (all-purpose) flour

Put the potatoes in a large pan and cover with cold water. Bring to a simmer and cook until tender, then drain in a colander. Once drained, tip the potatoes back into a dry pan and place over a low heat until dry. Crush with a fork (it's okay if it's a little lumpy) and set aside.

Heat the olive oil in a frying pan over a low heat and add the garlic. Gently cook for a few minutes until the garlic is aromatic and then add the sliced cabbage and water. Cook gently without colouring until the cabbage is soft and the water has evaporated, about 10 minutes. Stir from time to time to make sure it doesn't colour at all.

Remove from the heat and combine in a bowl with the potato. Add salt to taste then mash the potato and cabbage together until well combined. Set aside to cool. Divide the potato mixture into eight and shape into small round patties about 2.5 cm (1 in) thick. Put the patties on a plate, cover with cling film (plastic wrap) and refrigerate for at least 1 hour to firm up.

Heat a film of olive oil in a non-stick frying pan over a medium heat. Dust the top and bottom of the patties with flour making sure to brush off any excess. Cook the patties in the hot oil for about 5 minutes on each side, until golden and heated through.

Green vegetables and artichokes in jamón broth

Barazki-menestra

Menestra de verduras

A type of vegetable stew, *menestra de verduras* is a perfect accompaniment to meat or fish. I serve it in spring when the mixture of green vegetables are at their best, along with tender spring lamb cutlets or grilled salmon or trout. The vegetables in this recipe are really only a guide so feel free to use any mix you want or even just use one type of vegetable – as long as it's at its peak of freshness. The addition of jamón serrano adds a lovely meatiness to the dish and body to the sauce. In Spain it's usual for a menestra de verduras to be cooked until the vegetables are quite soft, but I like to cook the vegetables to a minimum to keep their vibrant colour and a bit of crunch.

Green vegetables and artichokes in jamón broth

Serves 4 as a tapa or sharing dish

15 ml (1 tablespoon) olive oil

50 g (1¾ oz) jamón serrano, diced

1 clove garlic, peeled and finely sliced

½ small onion, peeled and cut into a large dice

5 cm (2 in) length leek, white part only, rinsed and roughly chopped

300 ml (10 fl oz) vegetable stock

Coarse sea salt

50 ml (1½ fl oz) white wine

100 g (3½ oz) runner (green) beans, sliced at
    an angle into 5 cm (2 in) lengths

100 g (3½ oz) broad (fava) beans, shelled

100 g (3½ oz) fine green beans, cut in half

50 g (1¾ oz) peas

1 celery stalk, finely sliced at an angle

5 baby artichokes cooked and cut into quarters (see Basics) or 1 x 400 g
    (14 oz) can artichoke hearts drained and cut into quarters

1 teaspoon plain (all-purpose) flour

First make the broth. Heat the olive oil in a pan over medium heat and add the diced jamón serrano. Sauté till slightly golden, then take half of the jamón from the pan and set aside.

Add the garlic, onion and leek to the pan and sweat down until soft and translucent. Add the white wine and simmer until syrupy. Sprinkle over the flour, stirring in to avoid any lumps forming. Stir in the stock with a sprinkling of salt to taste, and bring to a gentle simmer. Cook gently for 15 minutes then pass through a fine sieve and discard the solids.

Bring a large pot of water to the boil and blanch the runner beans in it for 3 minutes. Remove them from the boiling water and plunge into a large bowl of iced water to halt the cooking process. Repeat with the broad beans, green beans and peas. Repeat with the celery but only blanch for 1 minute before plunging into the iced water. Tip the blanched vegetables into a colander to drain.

To serve, heat the broth to a simmer in a shallow pan and add the vegetables, stirring to combine. Cover with a lid and simmer for 2–3 minutes, shaking the pan often to heat the vegetables evenly. Stir in the reserved fried jamón and serve in a large shallow bowl, with crusty bread to soak up the broth.

Grilled asparagus with romesco sauce

Zainzuriak plantxan romesko saltsarekin

Espárragos a la plancha con salsa romesco

Romesco sauce works really well with grilled vegetables, especially asparagus where the contrasting colour looks great when presented on a platter. The smokiness of the romesco sauce also complements the flavour of chargrilled baby leeks or spring onions perfectly. Blanching the vegetables first isn't entirely necessary but it will help them grill more quickly and also preserves their colour.

Grilled asparagus with romesco sauce

SERVES 4 AS A SIDE DISH OR TAPA

2 bunches asparagus (about 24 spears)
250 ml (8½ oz) romesco sauce (see Basics)
30 ml (2 tablespoons) olive oil
Coarse sea salt

Trim and discard the woody base of the asparagus. Bring a large pot of water to the boil. Blanch the asparagus spears for 3 minutes then plunge into a bowl of iced water to cool. Drain in a colander and pat dry with a paper towel.

Gently heat the romesco sauce in a pan over a low heat. Keep warm while grilling the asparagus. Heat a grill pan over high heat. Gently toss the asparagus with the olive oil to coat and when the pan is nearly smoking hot, grill the asparagus for 1 minute on each side before transferring to a serving dish. Sprinkle with coarse sea salt and spoon the warm romesco sauce over the asparagus.

Potatoes cooked with onion and red pepper

Panadera patatak

Patatas panadera

Patatas panadera is a common method of cooking potatoes throughout Spanish households and restaurants. Onions and sometimes peppers are cooked slowly until soft and sweet then stirred through sautéed potatoes for a simple side dish that goes well with any meat or fish. There are many versions and techniques to make patatas panadera but this version is simple and fast to prepare.

Potatoes cooked with onion and red pepper

SERVES 4

60 ml (4 tablespoons) olive oil
1 medium onion, peeled and finely sliced
2 garlic cloves, finely sliced
1 red bell pepper (capsicum), de-seeded and sliced
1 green bell pepper (capsicum), de-seeded and sliced
1 bay leaf
1 kg (2¼ lb) baby new potatoes, peeled and cut into 1 cm (½ in)-thick slices
Coarse sea salt

Heat 30 ml (2 tablespoons) of the olive oil in a pan and add the onion and garlic. Cook, stirring constantly until slightly golden, then add the red and green peppers and bay leaf. Reduce the heat and continue to cook, stirring every few minutes, until the peppers are soft, about 15 minutes.

Meanwhile, put the potatoes in a large pan with a sprinkling of salt and cover with cold water. Bring to a simmer and cook until just tender. Drain thoroughly.

Heat the remaining olive oil in a large non-stick frying pan and add the potatoes. Sauté until the edges are golden. Add the onion and pepper mixture and toss together and continue cooking for a few more minutes to heat through.

Season with salt and serve on a flat platter as a side to fish or meat.

Roasted pepper and tomato salad with lentils and sherry vinegar

Piper erre entsalada dilista eta jerez ozpinarekin

Ensalada de asadillos con lentejas al jerez con lentejas y vinagre de jerez

They really do love peppers in Spain and have created many variations of warm and cold salads, around charred or roasted peppers. The charring imparts the flesh with a warm, smoky flavour and also makes it easy to remove the skin from the sweet melt-in-the-mouth pepper flesh. The roast tomatoes add a touch of much needed acidity to the dish and my addition of lentils adds a lovely earthy flavour and texture. *Asadillo* really benefits from sitting for a while to let the flavours meld so prepare it in advance. If you refrigerate your salad, bring it back to room temperature before serving. Serve as a side salad or with grilled red meat or fish.

Roasted pepper and tomato salad with lentils and sherry vinegar

SERVES 4

2 small onions, cut into wedges (keep the root end attached so
the layers don't separate)
10 garlic cloves, unpeeled
Olive oil, for drizzling
Coarse sea salt
2 red bell peppers (capsicum)
2 yellow bell peppers (capsicum)
2 plum tomatoes, each cut into 8 wedges
100 g (3½ oz) green Puy lentils, cooked (see Basics)
60 ml (4 tablespoons) sherry vinegar
1 teaspoon ground cumin
80 ml (2¾ fl oz) extra virgin olive oil
Small handful flat leaf parsley, shredded

Preheat your oven to 190°C/375°F/Gas mark 5.

Arrange a piece of kitchen foil on the work surface and place the onion wedges and garlic cloves on top. Drizzle with a little olive oil and a sprinkling of salt then fold in the edges to make an airtight parcel.

Place the red and yellow peppers on a baking tray and drizzle with a little olive oil. Roast in the oven along with the foil parcel for 25 minutes or until the skins are starting to blacken. Remove the peppers and the foil parcel from the oven. Put the peppers in a bowl and cover tightly with cling film (plastic wrap). The peppers will continue to steam so the skin will come off easily.

Once cool enough to handle, peel off the pepper skins with a small sharp knife and discard. Discard the seeds and tear the flesh into thick strips. Put the pepper strips in a large bowl. Unwrap the foil parcel and add the roast onions along with any juices. Squeeze the soft garlic flesh from the skins and add to the peppers and onions.

Add the lentils, vinegar, cumin, extra virgin olive oil and parsley with a sprinkling of sea salt and toss together. Leave for 30 minutes for the flavours to mingle before serving at room temperature.

Potatoes roasted in pork fat with red mojo sauce

Patata erreak iberiar-urdai eta mojo gorriarekin

Patatas asadas en tocino ibérico con mojo rojo

Potatoes roasted in duck fat taste fabulous, but they're even better when roasted in pig fat (*tocino ibérico*). Available in slabs from good Spanish delicatessens, tocino ibérico is the salted back fat from Iberian pigs, which are fed on acorns. The fat has a wonderful flavour. If you have trouble finding it, most Italian delis stock a similar product called *lardo*, which is an acceptable substitute.

The zingy *mojo rojo* works fantastically with these potatoes, transforming them into a kind of *patatas bravas* that can be served as a tapa or a side to simple roast meat dishes.

SERVES 4 AS A SIDE DISH OR TAPA

> *1 kg (2¼ lb) floury potatoes, peeled and cut into walnut-sized chunks*
> *100 g (3½ oz) salted tocino ibérico (salted pork back fat),*
>   *sliced into a few pieces*
> *4 cloves garlic, unpeeled*
> *1 bay leaf*
> *Coarse sea salt*
> *200 ml (7 fl oz) mojo rojo (see Basics)*

Put the potato chunks in a pan and cover with cold water. Bring to a simmer and cook for about 10 minutes or until the edges of the potatoes start to break up a little; drain into a colander.

Preheat the oven to 190°C/375°F/Gas mark 5 and put a roasting tray large enough to hold the potatoes in the oven.

Put the tocino ibérico in a frying pan and melt over a low heat. Increase the heat to medium-high and add the garlic cloves and bay leaf. Once the garlic is aromatic, add the potatoes to the pan. Turn the potatoes to coat them completely in the fat and cook for 3–4 minutes until they start to take on a little colour.

Remove the roasting tray from the oven and arrange the potatoes, bay leaf and garlic in the tray. Pour over any fat and sprinkle with coarse sea salt. Return the potatoes to the oven and roast for 10–15 minutes. Remove the tray from the oven, toss the potatoes and return to the oven for another 10–15 minutes or until the potatoes are golden and crisp.

Pour off the excess fat from the potatoes and serve in a dish with the mojo rojo sauce drizzled over.

Roast sweet potatoes with smoked paprika and sour cream

Batata erreak piperrauts ketu eta esnegain mingarrarekin

Batatas asadas con pimentón ahumado y nata agria

Roasted to intensify its sweetness and coated in maize flour for added crispness, these sweet potato wedges are truly delicious. A light dusting of smoked and hot paprika adds zing, which is complemented perfectly with cool sour cream to dip. Serve on their own or as an accompaniment to roast chicken or lamb.

SERVES 4

600 g (1 lb 5 oz) small sweet potatoes, peeled and cut into wedges
60 ml (4 tablespoons) olive oil
1 teaspoon fine sea salt
2 teaspoons smoked paprika
1 teaspoon hot paprika
2 tablespoons fine white maize flour (see pantry)
2 tablespoons finely chopped chives
200 ml (7 fl oz) sour cream

Preheat the oven to 180°C/350°F/Gas mark 4.

Place the sweet potato wedges in a bowl and drizzle with half the olive oil. Add a sprinkling of sea salt and toss to coat. Spread the wedges on a roasting tray lined with baking paper and roast in the oven for 20 minutes.

Meanwhile, combine the smoked and hot paprika, maize flour and salt.

After 20 minutes, remove the partly cooked wedges from the oven and increase the heat to 200°C/400°F/Gas mark 6.

Tip the wedges into a bowl, add the remaining olive oil and toss to coat. Sprinkle over the dry mix while tossing the bowl to coat the wedges evenly, and spread on the roasting tray.

Return the wedges to the oven and roast for 10 minutes or until they are starting to crisp. Turn the wedges over, then roast for another 10 minutes until golden and crisp.

Serve on a flat plate scattered with chopped chives, with sour cream spooned over the top or on the side.

Creamed potatoes

Patata-purea

Puré de patatas

Homely, comforting and rich, a good bowl of creamed potatoes is easy to make as long as you follow a few simple rules. Make sure to use the right potatoes, something floury such as King Edward or Desiree, which will soak up a lot of butter and milk without going greasy.

Make sure the potatoes are cut into even-sized chunks so they cook evenly. Once the cooked potatoes are drained return them to a dry pan and stir for a few minutes over a low heat to remove any excess moisture. Finally, cut the butter into cubes and add it to the potato while whisking. Or, if you prefer, add olive oil to the mash instead of the butter, for a healthier option.

SERVES 4

1 kg (2¼ lb) floury potatoes, peeled and cut into even chunks
80 g (2¾ oz) chilled butter, diced
200 ml (7 fl oz) milk
Coarse sea salt
Finely ground white pepper

Put the potatoes in a large pan, cover with cold water and bring to a boil over a high heat, then reduce to a simmer. Cook until tender but not falling apart. You should be able to crush the potatoes easily with the back of a fork.

Drain the potatoes thoroughly in a colander and return to the pan over a low heat. Stir for a few minutes to steam off any excess moisture and ensure the potatoes don't stick to the pan. The drier the potatoes, the lighter and fluffier the mash. Mash the potatoes until they are light and fluffy. Return the potato to a low heat and fold in the butter and milk until emulsified into the potato.

Season with a sprinkling of salt and white pepper before serving.

RICE

Arroza

ARROZ

IT'S SURPRISING FOR A COUNTRY THAT ONLY PRODUCES A SMALL AMOUNT of rice that one of its most iconic dishes happens to be made from the stuff. An authentic paella is truly a thing of beauty. Traditionally paella would be cooked outdoors over an open fire. Cooking a great paella is an art, and I recommend using a proper paella pan, although a large oven-safe frying pan is adequate.

Paella rice should be cooked *al dente*, and the grains should separate when cooked. There should be a dark crust on the bottom of the pan which adds a hint of smoky flavour to the final dish. If the rice isn't fully cooked once all the stock has been absorbed, sprinkle a little more hot stock over then cover with foil and return to the oven for a couple of minutes. The resulting steam will finish cooking the grains.

In the family home much wetter, soupier versions of paellas called *caldosos* are often prepared and can be cooked in any pan. Caldosos also require less care and attention to prepare, making them perfect for the home cook.

Paella with quail, mushrooms and jamón serrano

Galeper, onddo eta urdaiazpiko paella

Paella de codornices, setas y jamón serrano

Quail and jamón serrano are a perfect match and work fantastically with the mushrooms in this lovely paella. At home I like to bone the quail so I can make stock; however, quail are fiddly little birds, so any good butcher will do this task for you. This paella tastes great when made with boneless chicken thighs instead of quail. Just add to the pan when the quail legs usually go in and continue with the recipe.

Paella with quail, mushrooms and jamón serrano

SERVES 4

1 litre (1¾ pints) white chicken (or quail) stock
15 ml (1 tablespoon) olive oil
4 quail, boned, so you have 8 legs and 8 breasts
40 g (1½ oz) jamón serrano, finely chopped
150 g (5 oz) oyster mushrooms
1 small onion, finely diced
30 ml (2 tablespoons) aceite de ajo y perejil (see Basics)
300 g (10 oz) Bomba rice
Coarse sea salt

Preheat your oven to 160°C/325°F/Gas mark 3.

Heat the chicken stock to a bare simmer and keep hot. Heat the olive oil in a 30 cm (12 in) paella pan over medium heat. Add the quail breasts skin side down and cook for 1 minute or just until the skin is golden. Remove from the pan and set aside. Add the quail legs to the pan and sauté on both sides until golden then add the jamón serrano and keep cooking until it releases its fat. Add the mushrooms, onion and *aceite de ajo y perejil* then continue cooking until the onions are softened. Add the rice to the pan and continue cooking while stirring until the rice turns translucent.

Pour in the hot chicken stock with a sprinkling of coarse sea salt then stir and bring to the boil. Simmer rapidly for 5 minutes then transfer the pan to the preheated oven and bake for another 12–14 minutes until the rice is just about done.

Remove the pan from the oven and arrange the quail breasts, skin side up on top of the rice. Return to the oven for another 4 minutes to cook the breast. The breasts should still be pink when serving. Remove the pan from the oven then cover with a lid or foil and leave to rest for 5 minutes before serving.

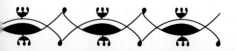

Egg-topped paella with artichokes, asparagus and morels

Orburu, zainzuri eta onddo paella arrautzarekin

Paella en costra con alcachofas, esparragos y setas

This is an interesting paella in which egg is poured over the top of the other ingredients for the last few minutes of cooking, forming a soft omelette-like coating over the rice. You do need to take care as the egg will turn rubbery if it is cooked for too long, so make sure the rice is cooked before adding the beaten eggs. If you want to make this really special, shave some fresh truffle over the top before serving. You can use any mushroom but morels work perfectly with the asparagus and egg. Buy fresh if you can, but dry morels are also a really good product so don't worry if that's all you can find. Just make sure to give them a good soak and rinse to wash off any grit.

Serves 4

> *1 bunch of asparagus (about 12 spears)*
> *1 litre (1¾ pints) vegetable stock*
> *15 ml (1 tablespoon) olive oil*
> *1 medium onion, finely diced*
> *100 g (3½ oz) morel mushrooms*
> *300 g (10 oz) Bomba rice*
> *30 ml (2 tablespoons) aceite de ajo y perejil (see Basics)*
> *6 baby artichokes cooked and cut into quarters (see Basics) or*
>   *1 x 400 g (14 oz) can artichoke hearts, drained and cut into quarters*
> *6 eggs, lightly beaten*
> *Coarse sea salt*

Preheat the oven to 160°C/325°F/Gas mark 3.

Trim and discard the woody base from the asparagus. Cut the spears in half and reserve the tips. Cut the remainder of the stem into 1 cm (½ in) pieces.

In a large pan heat the vegetable stock to a bare simmer and keep hot. Heat the olive oil over medium heat in a 30 cm (12 in) paella pan then add the onion and sweat down until soft. Add the morels and small pieces of asparagus then continue sweating down for another 2 minutes. Add the rice to the pan and continue cooking while stirring until the rice turns translucent. Stir in the *aceite de ajo y perejil* then pour in the hot vegetable stock with a good sprinkling of sea salt and bring to the boil. Simmer rapidly for 5 minutes then arrange the asparagus tips and artichokes in a neat pattern on the top of the rice. Transfer the pan to the preheated oven and bake for 12–14 minutes or until the rice is cooked.

Turn the oven up to 200°C/400°F/Gas mark 6 and remove the rice from the oven. Pour the beaten egg in an even layer over the rice then return to the oven.

Bake for another 4–5 minutes or until the egg is just set, then remove from the oven and leave to rest for 3–4 minutes before serving.

Wet rice with meatballs

Arroz saldatsua haragi-bolekin

Arroz caldoso con albondigas

Everyone loves meatballs, especially when cooked in a rich tomato-based sauce and served over pasta or rice. Similar to a paella, a *caldoso* is wetter and almost soupy in consistency so don't worry about all the extra liquid that's left once the rice is cooked, it's meant to be like that. In Spain this type of rice dish is actually more common than paella in the family home as it can be cooked in just about any pan on the stovetop and the cooking process is easier for the home cook. In this homely caldoso, the meatballs are cooked together with the rice so all the flavours meld together creating a hearty and fulfilling winter dinner.

Wet rice with meatballs

SERVES 4

30 ml (2 tablespoons) olive oil
1 garlic clove, peeled and finely chopped
½ small onion, peeled and finely chopped
200 g (7 oz) pork mince
200 g (7 oz) beef mince

RICE
30 ml (2 tablespoons) olive oil
1 small onion, finely diced
1 garlic clove, peeled and finely sliced
½ teaspoon sweet paprika
4 plum tomatoes, de-seeded and roughly chopped
120 g (4¼ oz) sofrito (see Basics)
1.5 litres (2¾ pints) white chicken stock (see Basics)
200 g (7 oz) Bomba rice
Small handful flat leaf parsley, finely chopped
Coarse sea salt

Heat the olive oil in a frying pan over medium heat. Add the garlic and onion and sweat down until soft. Scrape the mixture into a bowl. Leave to cool then add both minces with some salt. Use your hands to combine the ingredients. Measure tablespoons of the mix and roll into tight balls. Refrigerate for 20 minutes to firm up.

For the rice, heat the olive oil in a deep frying pan over medium–high heat. Add the meatballs and lightly brown all over. Remove from the pan and reserve. Add the onion and garlic and sweat down for a couple of minutes until soft. Stir in the paprika and tomatoes, then simmer until reduced and pulpy, about 10 minutes.

Stir in the *sofrito*, some salt and the stock. Bring to the boil. Stir in the rice, turn the heat down and simmer for 10 minutes. Add the meatballs and simmer for another 10 minutes or until the rice is cooked. Stir in the parsley. Serve immediately.

Paella with chorizo, morcilla and wood-roasted peppers

Txorizo, odolki eta piper-erre paella

Paella con chorizo, morcilla y pimientos asados

Probably the most recognisable Spanish ingredient, chorizo is included in literally thousands of regional dishes throughout the country. Morcilla is another common sausage popular in the Basque region. Both work perfectly in rice dishes where their spices and oils season the grains, flavouring the dish throughout, and in this paella the combination of both really gives it body. This is quite a heavy and warming paella more suited to the colder months of the year. For this paella I suggest using *morcilla con cebolla* instead of *morcilla de arroz* because it has a more pronounced flavour.

Paella with chorizo, morcilla and wood-roasted peppers

SERVES 4

1 litre (1¾ pints) white chicken stock
30 ml (2 tablespoons) olive oil
150 g (5 oz) morcilla con cebolla, cut into thick slices
150 g (5 oz) cooking chorizo, cut into thick slices
1 garlic clove, peeled and finely sliced
1 small onion, finely diced
300 g (10 oz) Bomba rice
120g (4½ oz) sofrito (see Basics)
1 teaspoon sweet smoked paprika
¼ teaspoon saffron threads
Coarse sea salt, for seasoning
6 piquillo peppers, drained of brine and cut in half

Preheat the oven to 160°C/325°F/Gas mark 3.

Heat the chicken stock to a low simmer and keep hot.

Heat the olive oil in a 30 cm (12 in) paella pan over medium heat. Add the morcilla and cook for 30 seconds to crisp up the skin. Remove from the pan and set aside. Add the chorizo to the pan and sauté till golden, remove from the pan. Add the garlic and onion to the pan and sauté while stirring for a few minutes until softened. Add the rice and continue to cook while stirring until the rice turns translucent, about 3 minutes.

Stir the *sofrito*, smoked paprika and saffron through the rice and pour over the hot stock. Add a sprinkling of salt, then simmer rapidly for 5 minutes over high heat. Arrange the chorizo, morcilla and piquillo peppers in a neat pattern on top of the rice then transfer to the oven and bake for 14–16 minutes, or until the rice is cooked through.

Remove the pan from the oven and cover the pan with a lid. Leave the paella to rest for 3–4 minutes before serving.

Paella cooked in prawn stock with fennel and alioli

Ganba-paella mihilu eta allioliarekin

Paella de gambas con hinojo y alioli

The best prawns I've ever tasted come from Spain. The most flavourful part of the prawn is the head and while eating in the most fantastic seafood restaurant Elkano, in the Basque town of Getaria, I observed the locals squeeze the juice from the heads over the tail flesh before popping it into their mouths. Once I tried it I understood why. It's such an explosion of intensely sweet prawn flavour, the perfect sauce.

Any paella needs a good stock and since prawn shells and heads are full of flavour, they are perfect for making a beautiful stock full of rich sea flavours. In this paella, the combination of sweet prawns and a slight aniseed flavour from the fennel match up fantastically and serving it with alioli adds an extra touch of luxury and richness.

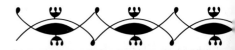

Paella cooked in prawn stock with fennel and alioli

SERVES 4

30 ml (2 tablespoons) olive oil
6 baby fennel, cut in half lengthways
1 small onion, finely diced
1 garlic clove, peeled and
   finely sliced
300 g (10 oz) Bomba rice
120 g (4½ oz) sofrito (see Basics)
180 ml (6 fl oz) alioli, to serve
   (see Basics)
Coarse sea salt

PRAWN STOCK
12 raw large prawns
30 ml (2 tablespoons) olive oil
1 small onion, peeled and diced
1 celery stalk, roughly chopped
1 medium carrot, peeled and diced
1 garlic clove, peeled
200 ml (7 fl oz) dry white wine
2 plum tomatoes, roughly chopped
1.2 litres (2 pints) fish stock

To make the stock, shell the prawns, leaving the small tail flaps on. Retain the heads and shells. Heat the olive oil in a pan over medium heat then add the prawn shells and heads and sauté for 2–3 minutes or until bright red and fragrant. Add the onion, celery, carrot and garlic and cook until the vegetables have taken on a little colour. Add the white wine and bring to a simmer, then reduce by half. Add the tomatoes and keep cooking until reduced by half again. Add the stock and bring it to the boil, skimming off any scum from the top. Reduce the heat to a gentle simmer and cook for 25 minutes.

Pass the stock through a fine sieve making sure to press the solids with the back of a spoon to extract as much liquid as possible. Discard the solids. You should have about 1 litre (1¾ pints) in total. If not top it up with water. Place the prawn stock back over a low heat to keep it hot.

Preheat the oven to 160°C/325°F/Gas mark 3.

For the paella, heat the olive oil in a 30 cm (12 in) paella pan over medium heat. Sauté the baby fennel on each side until slightly golden and remove from the pan. Put the onion and garlic in the pan and sweat down until soft. Add the rice and continue cooking while stirring until the rice turns translucent. Stir in the *sofrito*. Add the hot prawn stock with a good sprinkling of sea salt then stir and bring to the boil. Simmer rapidly for 5 minutes then arrange the baby fennel in a star shape on the top of the rice. Put the pan in the preheated oven and bake for 12–14 minutes until the rice is almost done.

Remove the pan from the oven and arrange the prawns on top of the rice. Return to the oven for another 3–4 minutes to cook the prawns.

Remove the pan from the oven and cover with a lid or aluminium foil and leave to rest for 3–4 minutes before serving with the alioli on the side.

FISH & SHELLFISH

Arrainak eta Itsaskiak

PESCADOS Y MARISCOS

THE BASQUES HAVE ALWAYS BEEN GREAT SEA-GOING PEOPLE and were making regular fishing voyagers to the cod-rich North Sea as early as the first half of the 16th century. But cod, although extremely popular in Spain where its flaky flesh is common place on every dining table in the country, is only a small part of Spain's love affair with seafood. Anyone who's been lucky enough to wander around any of Spain's fish markets will have seen the huge assortment of fish and shellfish regularly consumed, with many species considered delicacies.

The Spanish like their food cooked simply and many of the country's most popular seafood dishes are usually a simple affair. Many such as the Basque *marmitako* or Catalan *suquet* have their origins in traditional fisherman's meals prepared and eaten at sea. These dishes have found their way into top restaurants where bold young chefs cook them in the traditional manner but with modern techniques of refinement.

When sourcing seafood a local fishmonger will help you choose and prepare your fish and may also offer advice on the best way to cook your selection. I avoid frozen seafood except for octopus and squid.

Whatever seafood I do eat, I try to make sure it's a sustainable species, caught in an ethical manner.

Catalan fish stew of monkfish, prawns, mussels and clams

Suquet

Suquet

I first encountered *suquet* when I was lucky enough to cook at the acclaimed restaurant El Celler De Can Roca in Catalonia during my appearance on Professional MasterChef. Apart from being barely able to contain my excitement at such an opportunity I did my best to pick up as much knowledge as possible. One of the dishes I had to prepare was red mullet served with suquet sauce, demonstrated to me by the legendary Joan Roca. My version is a little more rustic and suited to the home cook, but it still does the dish justice and I'm sure Joan would approve!

Suquet is really quick and simple to put together once you have the *sofrito* and *picada* prepared. You can prepare both the day before you need it, making this a perfect dinner party dish that can be finished off in a matter of minutes.

Catalan fish stew of monkfish, prawns, mussels and clams

SERVES 4

120 g (4½ oz) sofrito (see Basics) puréed until smooth
75 ml (5 tablespoons) brandy
350 g (12 oz) baby new potatoes, peeled and cut into 5 mm (¼ in) slices
600 ml (1 pint) fish stock
50 g (2 oz) picada (see Basics)
200 g (7 oz) monkfish, cut into 4 pieces
4 red mullet fillets, about 40 g (1½ oz) each, boned and cut in half
12 prawns
12 mussels, de-bearded and cleaned
20 clams, purged, see pantry
Small handful flat leaf parsley, finely chopped

Heat the *sofrito* in a frying pan over medium heat, add the brandy and simmer for about 30 seconds to burn off the alcohol.

Add the potatoes and stock to the pan and bring to a simmer for about 10 minutes or until the potatoes are just tender. Stir in the *picada* and continue simmering for another 2–3 minutes, until the sauce thickens.

Add the monkfish, red mullet, prawns, mussels and clams to the sauce then place a lid over the frying pan. Continue to simmer for another 3–4 minutes until the mussels and clams have opened and the fish is cooked through.

If needed, add a little salt to the broth then stir in the parsley. Use a serving spoon to divide the fish and shellfish between four warm bowls then pour the broth over the top. Serve immediately with crusty bread to soak up the juices.

Salt cod, fennel and orange salad

Bakailao entsalada mihilu eta laranjarekin

Ensalada de bacalao con hinojo y naranja

Salt cod works surprisingly well with orange; the acidity and sweetness cuts into the salty cod. Making use of two of Spain's staple ingredients, this salad is popular on menus throughout the middle and south of Spain where its freshness is a blessing in the summer heat. I've stuck closely to tradition with my version except for the addition of fennel, which complements with the flavour of orange perfectly and also adds a lovely refreshing crunch.

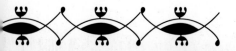

Salt cod, fennel and orange salad

SERVES 4

400 g (14 oz) salt cod, de-salinated (see Basics)
2 oranges
30 ml (2 tablespoons) orange juice (reserved from segmenting the oranges)
45 ml (3 tablespoons) white wine vinegar
80 ml (2¾ fl oz) extra virgin olive oil
½ small red onion, peeled and very finely sliced
1 small fennel bulb, finely sliced
80 g (3 oz) cured black olives, pitted
Good handful flat leaf parsley

Place the salt cod in a small pan and cover with cold water. Bring to a simmer and remove from the heat. Leave the cod in the water until cool enough to handle. In a large bowl, flake the cod into large pieces, discarding any skin and bones. Set aside.

Cut the top and bottom off the oranges then place on a chopping board. Remove the skin and white pith using a sharp knife. Working over a bowl to catch the juice, use a small sharp knife to cut each segment from between the membranes of the orange and reserve.

To make the dressing, whisk together the reserved orange juice with the white wine vinegar and olive oil.

Place the onion, fennel, orange segments, olives and parsley in the bowl with the cod, then pour over the dressing. Gently toss together and transfer to a serving dish. Serve chilled or at room temperature.

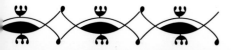

Basque stew of tuna in tomato and pepper sauce

Marmitakoa

Marmitako

I love *marmitako* and cook my own version in the same traditional way Basque fisherman have been doing for centuries. I make this dish with the potatoes cut with a rough edge, which releases more starch to thicken the sauce, so don't worry about the dish looking rustic, it will only taste better. Marmitako reheats really well so you can make it in advance, but make sure not to add the tuna until just before serving or it will overcook and turn dry.

Basque stew of tuna in tomato and pepper sauce

SERVES 4

45 ml (3 tablespoons) olive oil

1 small onion, peeled and finely chopped

2 garlic cloves, peeled and finely sliced

1 teaspoon sweet paprika

1 bay leaf

2 plum tomatoes, puréed until smooth

500 g (1¼ lb) starchy potatoes such as King Edward

1 green bell pepper (capsicum), deseeded and cut into strips

1 red bell pepper (capsicum), deseeded and cut into strips

800 ml (1½ pints) fish stock

Coarse sea salt

500 g (1¼ lb) tuna, cut into 2.5cm (1 in) cubes

Heat the olive oil in a wide pan over high heat. Add the onion and garlic and sweat down without colouring until soft and sticky, about 15 minutes. Add the paprika, bay leaf and tomatoes then stir to combine. Bring to a simmer and cook for about 10 minutes, stirring every few minutes, until the tomato mixture looks dry and sticky.

Peel the potatoes and, using a serrated knife, cut into 2.5 cm (1 in) cubes. Add the potatoes and peppers to the pan with the onion and garlic and pour over the fish stock. Bring to the boil, then reduce the heat to a simmer. Season with a sprinkling of sea salt and continue simmering for about 15 minutes or until the potatoes are soft but not falling apart.

Add the tuna chunks to the sauce and bring the sauce back to a simmer. As soon as it starts to bubble remove from the heat and cover with a lid. Leave to sit for 10 minutes before serving. Serve with crusty bread to soak up the wonderful juices.

Seared gurnard on tomato, potato and chorizo broth

Perloia plantxan tomate, patata eta txorizo saltsarekin

Bejel a la plancha en guiso de tomate, patata y chorizo

Economical, tasty and highly sustainable, gurnard is finally becoming more available. For a long time gurnard has been treated as a 'substitute' fish not useful for much other than bait, but chefs and the public alike are starting to discover its value in the kitchen. Gurnard holds its own when matched with strong flavours as in this simple dish, where a simple stew or *guiso* of tomato and potato flavoured with chorizo make a surprising but balanced match. If you can't find gurnard, try red mullet or a fine-textured fish such as sea bass.

Serves 4

1 x 400 g (14 oz) can of chopped tomatoes
1 bay leaf
100 ml (3½ fl oz) dry white wine
700 ml (1¼ pints) fish stock
800 g (1¾ lb) baby new potatoes, peeled
30 ml (2 tablespoons) light olive oil
100 g (3½ oz) cooking chorizo, cut into a pea-sized dice
1 garlic clove, peeled and finely chopped
1 small onion, finely diced
Coarse sea salt
4 grey or red gurnard fillets (about 150–160 g/5½ oz each)
Small handful of flat leaf parsley, finely chopped

Put the tomatoes, bay leaf, white wine and fish stock in a pan and bring to a simmer. Cook for 10 minutes then pass through a fine sieve, pressing the solids with the back of a spoon to extract as much liquid as possible.

Put the potatoes in a large pan and cover with cold water. Bring to a simmer and cook until just tender. Drain. Cut into quarters lengthways when cool.

Heat half the olive oil in a pan over medium heat and add the chorizo. Sauté gently until it releases its oils and crisps up a bit. Add the garlic and continue cooking until aromatic, then add the onion, cooking until soft. Pour in the broth and bring to a simmer. Cook gently for 5 minutes, add the potatoes and salt to taste and bring back to a simmer. Remove from direct heat. Keep warm.

Heat the remaining olive oil in a pan over medium–high heat. Season the fish then place in the pan skin side down and cook for 2–3 minutes or until crisp. Cook about 70 per cent of the way through, turn over and cook for 1 minute to finish.

Divide the broth between four dishes. Put the fish on top and sprinkle with parsley.

Hake and clams in salsa verde with jamón serrano

Legatza saltsa berdean txirla eta urdaiazpikoarekin

Merluza en salsa verde con almejas y jamón serrano

The first time I visited the Basque region of Spain, my introduction to the cuisine was *Merluza en salsa verde* served by my girlfriend's mother for lunch.

Hake in salsa verde typifies the style of food that is eaten every day at home throughout the Basque region. Often a dish like this will be just one of three or four courses eaten for lunch. This dish works equally well with other white fish such as cod, pollack or monkfish.

Hake and clams in salsa verde with jamón serrano

SERVES 4 AS A STARTER

250 ml (8½ fl oz) fish stock
20 clams, purged (see Pantry)
30 ml (2 tablespoons) light olive oil
50 g (1¾ oz) serrano ham cut into pea-sized dice
2 garlic cloves, peeled and finely diced
½ small onion, peeled and finely diced
1 teaspoon plain (all-purpose) flour
80 ml (3 fl oz) dry white wine
Coarse sea salt
4 hake cutlets, skin on, each about 160–180 g (5½ oz)
125g (4oz) oosely packed parsley, stems removed and finely chopped
55 g (2 oz) peas

Place the fish stock into a pan, cover and bring to a simmer over high heat. Add the clams, cover and simmer for 4–5 minutes or until all have opened. Drain through a fine sieve and reserve the juices, discarding any clams that have not opened.

Heat the olive oil in a non-stick frying pan over medium heat. Add the ham and gently sauté until just starting to colour. Add the garlic and onion and continue cooking until soft and translucent. Sprinkle over the flour and stir to combine. Pour the white wine into the pan, reduce the liquid to a glaze then slowly add the reserved clam cooking liquid, whisking to stop any lumps forming. Bring the sauce to a simmer and cook for 3–4 minutes. Season to taste.

Put the hake in the pan with the sauce and cover with a lid. Cook for 4–5 minutes, gently shaking the pan once or twice. Use a spatula to turn the cutlets, then scatter the parsley, peas and clams around the fish. Replace the lid and cook for another 2–3 minutes or until the hake is cooked. Serve straight from the pan or transfer the cutlets to a serving dish and pour over the sauce and clams.

Olive oil-poached cod with lentils, chorizo and piperade jus

Bakailaoa dilista, txorizo eta piperrada zukuarekin

Bacalao con lentejas, chorizo y jugo de piperrada

Gently poaching fish in olive oil gives it luscious soft flesh and preserves the natural flavour of the sea. This dish contains contrast between the sweet *piperrada*, the soft fish and bite from the earthy puy lentils. The chorizo brings it all together adding a little spicy meatiness. This really is simple rustic cooking but would comfortably sit on a menu in just about any fine-dining restaurant.

Olive oil-poached cod with lentils, chorizo and piperade jus

MAKES 4 ENTRÉE SIZED PORTIONS

250 g (9 oz) piperrada (see Vegetables)
200 ml (7 fl oz) fish stock
4 cod fillets, skin on (about 150–160 g/5½ oz each)
Coarse sea salt
600 ml (1¼ pints) light olive oil (or enough to cover the cod in a small pan)
2 garlic cloves, slightly crushed with the flat edge of a knife
1 bay leaf
100 g (3 ½ oz) cooking chorizo, cut into pea-sized dice
200 g (7 oz) Puy lentils, cooked (see Basics)
A few flat leaf parsley or small basil leaves, to serve

To prepare the piperade jus, place half the *piperrada* in a small pan with the fish stock and heat to a simmer. Transfer to a blender and purée till smooth. Pour back into the pan and keep warm. In a separate pan, heat the remaining *piperrada* and keep warm.

Season the fish and set aside. Meanwhile, place the olive oil in a small pan that will snugly hold the cod fillets. Add the garlic and bay leaf and place over a low heat. When it reaches 60°C/140°F slide the cod fillets into the olive oil. Bring the oil back to 60°C/140°F and leave for 8–10 minutes for the cod to gently poach. Test a piece by pressing it with the back of a spoon, it will start to flake when ready.

Prepare the lentils. Heat a small glug of olive oil in a frying pan set over medium heat. Sauté the chorizo until it is golden and has released its lovely oil. Reduce the heat to low. Add the lentils to the pan and gently heat through, stirring ocassionally.

To serve, divide the warm *piperrada* between four warm bowls and place the lentils on top. Gently lift the cod fillets from the oil, shake off the excess oil and place on top of the lentils. Pour the *piperrada* 'jus' around the fish and decorate with the basil or parsley leaves. Sprinkle the fish with a little coarse sea salt.

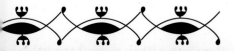

Whole fried red mullet with mojo verde

Barbarin frijituak mojo berdearekin

Salmonetes fritos con mojo verde

Whole fried fish is such a simple technique and delivers outstanding results. It should be more common in western cooking. Extremely popular throughout Asia, the Spanish seem to be the only Europeans who have mastered the technique in such dishes as *fritura Andaluza* where they serve an amazing assortment of fish lightly coated and fried.

After a dusting in flour the fish is fried in hot, clean oil, resulting in a beautifully moist but crispy-skinned fish that also looks great served with bright green *mojo verde*.

SERVES 4 AS A TAPAS OR SHARING DISH

4 whole red mullet, gutted and scaled, about 120 g (4 oz) each
1 litre (1¾ pints) vegetable oil, for frying
100 g (3½ oz) plain (all-purpose) flour
½ teaspoon coarse sea salt
300 ml (10½ fl oz) mojo verde (see Basics)
Small handful coriander leaves

Using a sharp knife, slash the fish four or five times on each side, cutting a little deeper into the thickest part of the fillet.

Pour the vegetable oil in a pan (or use a deep fryer if you have one) and heat to 180°C/350°F. If you don't have a fryer use a sugar thermometer to check the temperature of the oil, or drop a small piece of white bread in the oil, it should turn golden brown after 30 seconds.

Mix the flour and salt on a plate and dust the fish thoroughly, shaking off any excess flour. Carefully lower the fish, two at a time, into the hot oil and cook for 4–5 minutes until golden all over and cooked through. Transfer to paper towels to soak up any excess oil.

Spread the *mojo verde* on a flat serving dish then place the fish belly down on the sauce. Sprinkle over the coriander leaves and a little coarse sea salt.

Langoustine Russian salad

Entsalada errusiarra otarrainxkekin

Ensaladilla rusa de langostinos

Langoustine with mayonnaise is a classic combination, and when combined with a creamy Russian salad it's a match made in heaven. A must on any tapa menu, *ensaladilla rusa* changes slightly from region to region but is always based on potatoes dressed with some type of mayonnaise. As you head to the north of Spain ensaladilla rusa becomes more elaborate often containing asparagus, piquillo peppers and preserved tuna. Texture is important so make sure the ingredients are cooked until quite soft including the carrots. This is a fantastic side dish that works particularly well with the sweet flesh of langoustines, prawns or, even lobster, for a special occasion.

Langoustine Russian salad

SERVES 4 AS A TAPA OR SHARING DISH

> *12 langoustines or large prawns*
> *500 g (1¼ lb) waxy potatoes, peeled and cut into a pea-sized dice*
> *2 medium carrots, peeled and cut into a pea-sized dice*
> *100 g (3½ oz) fresh or frozen peas*
> *3 boiled eggs, diced*
> *20 g (¾ oz) green olives in brine, drained and sliced into thin rings*
> *180 ml (6 fl oz) mayonnaise (see Basics)*
> *1 lemon, cut into wedges*
> *Coarse sea salt*

If the langoustines are alive place them in the freezer for 1 hour before cooking. Bring a large pot of heavily salted water to the boil. Add the langoustines and boil for 2 minutes, drain. Place in a bowl and cover with cold water to chill, drain again and place in the refrigerator until serving.

Place the diced potato in a pan and cover with cold water. Add a sprinkling of salt, then bring to a simmer and cook the potatoes until tender but not falling apart. Drain into a colander and allow to cool.

Meanwhile, cook the diced carrot until tender in a pan of boiling water. Use a slotted spoon to transfer to a bowl of iced water. Cook the peas in the same water for a few minutes (or longer if they are fresh) and chill as before, then pour into a colander to drain. Pat the carrots, peas and potatoes dry with paper towel and put in a mixing bowl. Add the diced egg, sliced olives and the mayonnaise. Season, then gently fold together to coat evenly. Cover and refrigerate until ready to serve.

Transfer the Russian salad to a large flat serving dish and arrange the langoustines and lemon wedges around the edges.

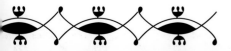

Fideo pasta with prawns, squid and cockles

Fideoak ganba, txirla eta txibiekin

Fideos con gambas, calamares y almejas

The nature of Basque hospitality always means that there will be a fantastic meal involved at family gatherings and this one is definitely appropriate to serve. You need the freshest prawns you can buy for this dish and make sure you leave the heads on when cooking. Then, when you eat, squeeze the juices out of the head and mix them into the dish. The flavour is amazing.

Fideo pasta with prawns, squid and cockles

SERVES 4

2 small squid, about 100 g (3½ oz) each
400 g (14 oz) dry fideo pasta
15 ml (1 tablespoon) olive oil
12 large raw prawns, shells removed but heads intact
1 small onion, finely chopped
100 ml (3½ fl oz) dry white wine
45 ml (3 tablespoons) aceite de ajo y perejil (see Basics)
24 clams, purged, see pantry
Coarse sea salt

To prepare the squid pull the head and tentacles away from the body. Cut off the part of the head with the eyes and discard. Where the tentacles join there is a hard 'beak', cut this out and discard. Separate the tentacles and set aside. Pull the two 'wings' off the squid tube and discard. Remove and discard the long thin cartilage from inside the squid tube. Scrape the darkish skin from the outside of the squid, and cut the tube into 5 mm (¼ in)-wide rings.

Bring a large pan of salted water to the boil over high heat. Add the fideo and cook for about 6–7 minutes.

Meanwhile, heat the olive oil in a frying pan over medium–high heat, add the squid and prawns and sauté for 20 seconds. Remove from the pan and set aside. Reduce the heat to medium then add the onion and sweat down until soft. Add the white wine and boil for about a minute to burn off the alcohol.

Add the *aceite de ajo y perejil* and clams, then cover the pan and leave to cook until the clams have opened, about 3 minutes. Discard any that are unopen, then return the prawns and squid to the pan. Heat gently to cook through.

Drain the pasta in a colander and add to the frying pan with the sauce and seafood. Toss together and sprinkle with salt. Divide over warm plates and serve.

Seared salmon with prawns, butter bean bisque and alioli

Izozkina plantxan ganba eta babarrun fumetean allioliarekin

Salmón a la plancha en fumet de gambas con alubias y alioli

Prawn shells make a flavourful sauce to serve with just about any fish, in this case salmon and the prawns themselves. The heads are full of flavour which is brought out by sautéing them until bright red and aromatic then simmering briefly. Salmon holds up well to the strong flavours in this sauce, but the addition of creamy butter beans adds a mellow note. Before searing the salmon, dry the skin thoroughly. This will give you a delightful crispy skin.

Seared salmon with prawns, butter bean bisque and alioli

SERVES 4

2 plum tomatoes

15 ml (1 tablespoon) olive oil

1 small carrot, peeled and
finely diced

200 g (7 oz) dry butter (fava) beans, cooked
(see Basics) or 2 x 400 g (14 oz) cans of
cooked butter beans, drained and rinsed

4 salmon fillets skin on (about 150 g/
5 oz each)

Coarse sea salt

100 ml (3½ fl oz) alioli (see Basics)

Light olive oil, to drizzle

BROTH

15 ml (1 tablespoon) mild olive oil

12 raw large prawns, heads and shells re-
moved and reserved (leave the tail flaps
on for presentation)

1 garlic clove, peeled

½ small onion, peeled and chopped

½ small carrot, peeled and chopped

½ celery stalk, chopped

1 bay leaf

Small pinch of saffron

5 black peppercorns

100 ml (7 fl oz) white wine

1 tablespoon plain (all-purpose) flour

1 tablespoon tomato paste (purée)

400 ml (14 fl oz) water

Coarse sea salt

To make the broth, heat the olive oil in a pan over medium heat and add the prawn heads and shells. Sauté until deep red and aromatic, then add the garlic, onion, carrot, celery, bay leaf, saffron and peppercorns. Sweat down for a few minutes to soften the vegetables then add the white wine. Reduce until the wine has evaporated and the mixture is dry; sprinkle over the flour and stir to combine.

Add the tomato paste then slowly pour in the water, stirring to prevent any lumps forming, and bring back to a gentle simmer. Skim any scum from the top of the liquid and simmer gently for 20 minutes. Pass the stock through a fine sieve pressing the solids with a spoon to extract as much liquid as possible.

Bring a pot of water to the boil. Cut a cross into the top of the tomatoes and place into the boiling water for 20 seconds. Lift out with a slotted spoon and plunge straight into iced water to cool. Drain the tomatoes, and using a small knife, lift the skin from the tomatoes and peel. Cut the tomatoes into quarters and scoop out the seeds so you have eight 'petals'. Dice and set aside.

To finish the dish, heat the olive oil in a pan over a medium heat. Gently sauté the carrot without colouring until soft, then add the butter beans and prawn broth. Bring to a gentle simmer and cook for 2 minutes to heat the beans through. Season to taste, remove from direct heat and keep hot.

Heat a little light olive oil in a non-stick frying pan over medium heat. Make sure the salmon skin is completely dry by scraping it with a knife-edge until no more moisture comes out. Season with salt then place in the pan skin side down and leave to sear for about 3 minutes or until cooked about 70 per cent through. Turn the salmon over and add the prawns to the pan. Sear on both sides for about a minute, by then the salmon will be cooked through.

Add the tomato to the broth and stir through before transferring to a serving dish. Place the salmon on top, then arrange the prawns around. Spoon a little alioli on top of the salmon or serve on the side for everyone to help themselves.

POULTRY

Hergaztiak

AVES

WITH THE POPULARITY OF SEAFOOD AND PORK IN SPAIN it's no surprise that poultry almost takes a back seat in the country's cuisine. That's not to say the Spanish don't eat it – chicken, duck, quail and other game birds are popular in hunting regions such as Andalucía where shooting is a popular past time.

Chicken is commonly braised in a *chilindrón* or cooked *al ajillo* with copious amounts of garlic, or added to rice dishes and paellas. Small game birds may be roasted whole or cooked in escabeche where a vinegar-based sauce is used for flavour and also as a method of preservation.

Duck, although not hugely popular, is usually roasted or confit in the traditional French manner and served with fruit such as oranges, cherries or figs.

Chicken braised in sherry and garlic sauce

Oilaskoa baratxuriarekin

Pollo al ajillo

Popular in every region of Spain, *pollo al ajillo*, or chicken cooked with garlic, seems to be a requisite on every tapa menu outside of Spain. Marinated for hours to get the seasoning all the way through the chicken, then slowly braised until the chicken literally falls off the bone, you will realise why this dish is so popular when you taste it.

For this recipe you will need a large-based pan or casserole that will hold the chicken in a single layer.

Chicken braised in sherry and garlic sauce

SERVES 4

8 large chicken legs or thighs on the bone (or a mix)
Coarse sea salt
120 ml (4¾ oz) aceite de ajo y perejil (see Basics)
30 ml (2 tablespoons) olive oil
1 small onion, peeled and finely diced
2 bay leaves
250 ml (8½ fl oz) fino sherry
250 ml (8½ fl oz) white chicken stock (see Basics)
Small handful flat leaf parsley, finely chopped

Place the chicken pieces in a bowl, pour over the *aceite de ajo y perejil* and massage into the meat. Cover and leave in the refrigerator to marinate for at least 3 hours, or overnight, if you can.

Preheat the oven to 150°C/300°F/Gas mark 2.

Heat the olive oil in a large pan or casserole over a low to medium heat. Season the chicken pieces with salt and add to the pan, skin side down. Sear until the chicken is golden brown, about 5–6 minutes, being careful not to burn the garlic. Turn the chicken and sear on the other side for another 5 minutes. Remove from the pan and set aside on a plate. Reduce the heat slightly and add the onion and bay leaves. Gently sauté until the onion is soft and slightly golden, about 10 minutes.

Return the chicken to the pan, add the sherry and bring to a simmer. Reduce the liquid to a glaze, add the chicken stock and return the liquid to a simmer.

Place a disc of baking paper over the chicken and place in the oven to braise for 1 hour 30 minutes. This method ensures the chicken is protected from drying out, while the sauce reduces slightly. When cooked, the chicken should be very tender and pull away from the bone easily.

Transfer the chicken to a serving dish, pour over the juice and scatter over the chopped parsley, to serve.

Pan-fried quail with grapes, almond and sherry vinegar

Galeperrak mahats, almendra eta jerez-ozpinarekin

Codornices con uvas, almendras y vinagre de jerez

This is the perfect way to cook quail and takes just minutes from start to finish. Quail works so well with sweet ingredients like grapes and honey, and the addition of sherry vinegar to the dish gives a perfect balance of sweet and sour. Toasted almonds add an interesting crunch and are a lovely textural contrast to the tender quail. Serve this dish piping hot straight from the pan and don't be offended by everyone licking the delicious sauce from their fingers at the table.

Pan-fried quail with grapes, almond and sherry vinegar

Serves 4 as a sharing dish

20 g (¾ oz) flaked almonds
4 large whole quail
30 ml (2 tablespoon) olive oil
Coarse sea salt
15 ml (1 tablespoon) sherry vinegar
15 ml (1 tablespoon) honey
100 g (3½ oz) seedless green grapes, washed, dried and cut in half

Preheat the oven to 180°C/350°F/Gas mark 4.

Spread the almonds on a baking tray and roast for 6–7 minutes, or until golden.

To prepare the quails, use a sturdy pair of kitchen scissors or a sharp knife to cut down each side of the backbone. Discard the backbone then flatten the quail on a chopping board and cut through the breast bone to separate the two halves.

Heat half the olive oil in frying pan over medium heat. Season the quail halves with sea salt and add to the pan, skin side down. Cook for 3 minutes until golden brown, turn and cook for another 2 minutes on the other side. Test to see if it's cooked through, quail is best served a little pink.

Remove the quail from the pan, retaining any juices that remain.

Place the frying pan back on the heat and add the sherry vinegar and honey. As the liquid heats and bubbles scrape the bottom of the pan (de-glaze) to mix all the little bits that are full of flavour into the sauce.

Add the remaining olive oil and grapes and toss to warm through.

Arrange the quail on a serving dish then pour over the dressing.

Sprinkle over the almonds and season with salt.

Chicken with jamón, peppers and tomato

Arkumea txilindron eran

Pollo al chilindrón

The mountainous region of Aragón situated in northeast Spain is home to many rustic stews similar to this, commonly made with lamb, chicken or rabbit, and always including peppers, tomato and usually paprika. This simple chicken braise, or *pollo al chilindrón*, combines chicken with jamón serrano, which adds body and a meatiness to the sauce. Traditionally a *chilindrón* would be cooked in a large pot over an open fire, but my version is slowly braised in the oven until the meat falls off the bone. If you prefer lamb, simply replace the chicken with lamb neck fillets.

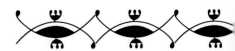

Chicken with jamón, peppers and tomato

SERVES 4

45 ml (3 tablespoons) olive oil

150 g (5 oz) jamón serrano, cut into thin strips

1 kg (2¼ lbs) chicken thighs or drumsticks (or a mix of both)
with skin and on the bone

3 garlic cloves, peeled and finely chopped

1 large onion, peeled and finely diced

2 red bell peppers (capsicum), deseeded, membrane removed, cut into
2.5 cm (1 in) strips

1 bay leaf

2 teaspoons sweet paprika

6 plum tomatoes, puréed until smooth in a food processor or blender

200 ml (7 fl oz) water

Coarse sea salt

Preheat the oven to 150°C/300°F/Gas mark 2.

In a casserole or large pan that will fit all the chicken in a single layer, heat the olive oil over medium–high heat. Add the jamón serrano and sauté until golden, then remove from the dish and set aside. Lightly season the chicken pieces, add to the pan and sauté on all sides until golden. Remove from the pan and set aside.

Add the garlic and onion to the hot oil then sauté, stirring, for a few minutes until soft and translucent. Add the red pepper, bay leaf and paprika and continue sautéing for another few minutes until soft. Pour the puréed tomato and water into the pan and heat to a gentle simmer. Allow to simmer for 10 minutes to reduce a little and for the flavours to come together.

Stir in the serrano ham and add the chicken pieces, skin side up, pushing the chicken into the liquid to cover. Slowly braise in the oven for 1 hour 30 minutes basting the chicken with the pan juices every 20 minutes or so. If the chicken looks like it's drying out, moisten with a few tablespoons of water. Once cooked, remove from the oven, cover and allow to rest for 10–15 minutes before serving with puréed potatoes or a simple green salad with crusty bread.

Roast guinea fowl with morcilla, apple, trinxat and onion-cider sauce

Pintada errea sagardo zukuan trinxat eta odolkiarekin

Pintada al horno a la sidra con morcilla y trinxat

Cider is popular across all the northern regions of Spain and each has its own distinct variety. The two that stand out are the sweet Asturian ciders and the dry, almost vinegary Basque varieties. I use both in cooking, though the sweeter varieties lend themselves to poultry and game perfectly. I served a dish similar to this to 30 Michelin-starred chefs during my time on Professional MasterChef with great results and I was blown away by the positive comments I received. *Trinxat* is the perfect accompaniment but if you want to make it a little more straightforward try it with *tocino ibérico* roast potatoes or even creamed potatoes.

Roast guinea fowl with morcilla, apple, trinxat and onion-cider sauce

SERVES 4

2 medium onions, peeled and cut into quarters
2 carrots, peeled and cut into chunks
500 ml (1 pint) brown chicken stock (see Basics)
250 ml (8 fl oz) sweet apple cider
6 sprigs of thyme
6 garlic cloves, peeled
1 whole guinea fowl
1 teaspoon coarse sea salt
30 ml (2 tablespoons) mild olive oil
2 green apples, peeled, cored and cut into wedges
8 trinxat patties (see Vegetables)
12 x 1.2 cm (½ in) slices of morcilla de arroz

Preheat the oven to 180°C/350°F/Gas mark 4.

Place the onion, carrot, stock, cider, 3 sprigs of thyme and 3 garlic cloves in a deep roasting pan and place a rack over the top.

Stuff the remaining garlic and thyme into the cavity of the guinea fowl and rub the skin with salt.

Massage half the olive oil into the guinea fowl then season on all sides with coarse sea salt. Place breast side up in the roasting pan on the rack, making sure it isn't touching the liquid.

Roast in the oven for 45–55 minutes or until the juices run clear when a knife is inserted between the leg and breast. Turn the guinea fowl over so it is breast side down, cover with foil and leave to rest in a warm place.

Meanwhile, tip the cooking liquid through a fine sieve into a pan, discarding the solids. Skim off any excess fat, bring to a simmer and reduce by half. Add the apple wedges to the reduced sauce and simmer until softened but not falling apart. Remove from the heat and keep warm.

While the sauce is reducing, heat a film of light olive oil in a non-stick frying pan. Add the *trinxat* patties and cook on each side for 3 minutes, until golden and heated through. Wipe out the pan, add a little more oil and sear the morcilla slices for 1 minute on each side until crisp. Place the guinea fowl on a serving dish with the morcilla slices. Spoon the apples and some of the sauce around the dish, reserving some of the sauce to serve separately. Serve the trinxat in a separate dish on the side.

Chicken braised with cannellini beans, tomato and chorizo

Babarrun txuriak oilasko, tomate eta txorizoarekin

Alubias blancas con pollo, tomate y chorizo

This is a lovely wintery dish that's quick to put together; it's just a matter of leaving it to braise slowly until it cooks to tender perfection. Rich and saucy *guisos* (stews) similar to this are commonplace through the Spanish Pyrenees, making the most of whatever is at hand. Chicken legs or thighs left on the bone and braised in an aromatic broth absorb flavour superbly and will stay moist unlike the breast, which has a tendency to dry out if over-cooked. Chorizo goes fantastically with chicken, and also adds a wonderful meaty, paprika richness to the sauce. Serve with some crusty bread to soak up all the wonderful juices.

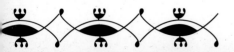

Chicken braised with cannellini beans, tomato and chorizo

SERVES 4

60 ml (4 tablespoons) olive oil

150 g (5 oz) cooking chorizo, cut into thick slices

8 large chicken legs or thighs (or a mix)

Coarse sea salt

3 garlic cloves, peeled and finely sliced

1 small onion, peeled and finely diced

1 bay leaf

4 sprigs thyme

200 ml (7 fl oz) full-bodied red wine

5 plum tomatoes, blitzed to a smooth purée in a food processor

200 g (7 oz) dry cannellini beans, cooked (see Basics) or 2 x 400 g (14 oz) cans of cooked cannellini beans, drained and rinsed

400 ml (14 fl oz) white chicken stock (see Basics)

Small handful sage leaves

Preheat the oven to 150°C/300°F/Gas mark 2. Heat half the olive oil in a heavy pan or casserole over medium–high heat. Add the chorizo slices and sauté until they release their oil and are golden on the edges. Use a slotted spoon to remove the chorizo from the casserole, leaving the oil, and set aside.

Reheat the casserole, season the chicken legs with sea salt and fry in the chorizo oil until well coloured. Remove the chicken from the pan and set aside.

Add the garlic, onion, bay and thyme to the oil and sauté until soft. Pour in the wine and reduce by half, then pour in the tomato purée and bring to a simmer. Leave the tomato sauce to simmer for 10–15 minutes or until reduced by about half.

Return the reserved chorizo and chicken back to the casserole along with the cooked cannellini beans and pour over the stock. Bring to a very gentle simmer and place in the preheated oven to braise for 1 hour 15 minutes.

Meanwhile, heat the remaining olive oil in a small frying pan over medium heat then add the sage leaves and sauté until crisp. Transfer to a paper towel to soak up any excess oil.

Once the chicken braise has cooked, remove from the oven and leave to rest for 10 minutes for the flavours to meld. Serve sprinkled with the crisp sage leaves.

Duck leg confit with butternut squash and sweet and sour figs

Ahate izter konfitatua zapallo-purea eta piku gazi-gezekin

Confit de pato con puré de zapallo e higos agridulces

Duck confit is delicious and simple to make ahead of time, to have in the refrigerator to finish off quickly, before serving. Once the duck is cooked you can put it in a container and pour the fat over the top. It will keep well chilled for more than a week, which will also improve its flavour. Most supermarkets now sell duck fat in jars or cans but if you have any problem finding it, your butcher should be able to order it for you.

Duck leg confit with butternut squash and sweet and sour fig

SERVES 4

4 teaspoons coarse sea salt, plus extra for seasoning

2 bay leaves, torn into small pieces

3 garlic cloves, peeled and sliced

1 teaspoon black peppercorns

6 thyme sprigs

4 duck legs

600 g (1¼ lb) duck fat

1 whole butternut squash, about 1 kg (2¼ lb)

30 ml (2 tablespoons) olive oil

15 ml (1 tablespoon) white wine vinegar

15 ml (1 tablespoon) honey

400 ml (14 fl oz) brown chicken stock (see Basics)

4 fresh figs, each cut into about 6 wedges

To marinate the duck, rub the salt, bay leaves, garlic, peppercorns and thyme into the duck legs then place in a non-metallic dish. Cover tightly with cling film (plastic wrap) and refrigerate overnight to marinate.

The next day, preheat the oven to 110°C/225°F/Gas mark ¼.

Peel the butternut, cut in half, scrape out the seeds with a spoon and discard. Cut the flesh into rough 2.5 cm (1 in) chunks and place in a large bowl with the oil and a sprinkling of salt. Toss to coat then arrange the pumpkin chunks in a single layer on a baking tray covered with baking paper. Cover tightly with aluminium foil, making sure to seal the edges so it's airtight so the butternut won't dry out during cooking. Brush the herbs, spices and garlic off the duck legs and discard.

Place the legs in a snug-fitting overnproof tray or pan then add the duck fat. Place over a low heat until the fat has melted then put in the oven along with the butternut squash. Cook for 3 hours, removing the butternut after 2 hours.

Place the butternut into a pan over a low heat and stir for a few minutes to steam dry. Use a potato masher to crush the butternut to a purée or process in a food processor until smooth. Set the butternut purée aside or chill until serving.

After 3 hours of cooking, the duck flesh will fall off the bone so it needs to be handled gently. Carefully lift the legs from the fat and place in a colander to drain. Pass the fat through a fine sieve and discard the solids. If serving later, place the duck in a clean non-metallic dish or jar, pour the fat over to cover and refrigerate until serving.

To finish the dish, preheat the oven to 350°F/180°C/Gas mark 4.

Place the butternut squash in a pan over a low heat to warm through. Heat a separate non-stick frying pan over medium heat. Remove the duck legs from the fat, place in the frying pan skin side down and sear until golden and crisp. Turn and repeat on the other side. Remove the duck from the frying pan and place in a roasting tray. Bake for 7–8 minutes to heat through. Discard any excess fat from the frying pan and place back on the heat. Add the vinegar and honey, leave to boil for a few moments then add the chicken stock and bring to a simmer. Reduce the liquid by half or until thickened, add the fig and simmer for a few more minutes to soften. Divide the butternut between four warm plates, place a confit duck leg on top and finish with a drizzle of the fig sauce over the top.

MEAT
Haragiak
CARNES

Bᴇᴇꜰ ᴀɴᴅ ʟᴀᴍʙ ᴀʀᴇ ʀᴇɢᴜʟᴀʀʟʏ ᴇᴀᴛᴇɴ ᴛʜʀᴏᴜɢʜᴏᴜᴛ Sᴘᴀɪɴ with most being reared in the north and northwest of the country where the green pastures are more suited to raising cattle and sheep.

Younger animals are usually simply grilled or roasted while older beasts are commonly braised al *chilindrón* in a rich sauce of tomatoes and peppers.

In the Basque Country beef is a specialty where huge ribeyes or chuletón, are grilled over charcoal then served on the bone with nothing more than a sprinkling of coarse sea salt and thinly sliced fried potatoes.

On the other hand, pork production is huge with a population of more than 25 million feeding the demand for chorizos, jamóns and other cured products. Most prized of all, the black Iberian pig, is commonly fed a diet solely of acorns which gives the meat a luscious richness and nutty flavour with a rich layer of fat. Fresh pork is grilled or roasted with a favourite dish being roast suckling pig or cochinillo asado, in which young piglets are roasted whole, producing crisp skin and luscious, gelatinous flesh.

Cheaper cuts of meat, with careful, slower cooking times, will reward you with an amazing flavour and melt–in-the-mouth texture."

Braised pork cheek in vizcaina sauce with creamed potato

Txerri-masailak bizkaitar erara patata-purearekin

Carrilleras de cerdo a la vizcaína con puré de patata

Vizcaina sauce is rich with peppers, tomatoes and in this dish, the cooking juices from the pork cheeks. This is traditional Basque cooking and all through the region you will find numerous dishes cooked with vizcaina sauce, most commonly salt cod followed by pork trotters and sometimes poultry. Here I've replaced the trotters with cheeks, which still deliver a great flavour and are a lot easier to prepare. Any cut that benefits from long, slow cooking will work well in this recipe, including lamb and beef. Just like other slow-cooked dishes it really does taste better reheated the day after cooking so plan ahead, if you can.

Braised pork cheek in vizcaina sauce with creamed potato

SERVES 4

30 ml (2 tablespoons) olive oil
1 kg (2¼ lbs) pork cheeks, trimmed of fat
Coarse sea salt
1 large onion, roughly chopped into
    large chunks
1 large carrot, peeled and roughly chopped
3 garlic cloves, peeled
1 bay leaf
1 tablespoon sweet paprika
200 ml (7 fl oz) red Rioja or full-
    bodied red wine
500 ml (1 pint) White Chicken Stock
    (see Basics)

VIZCAINA SAUCE BASE

45 ml (3 tablespoons) light olive oil
20 g (¾ oz) stale white bread, torn into
    fingernail-sized pieces
3 garlic cloves, peeled and
    finely sliced
1 large onion, peeled and chopped
    into quarters
1 red bell pepper (capsicum), seeded and
    roughly diced
2 plum tomatoes, chopped
1 tablespoon sweet paprika
1 teaspoon hot paprika

TO SERVE
Creamed potatoes (see Basics)

Preheat the oven to 120°C/250°F/Gas mark ½.

Heat the olive oil in a sturdy lidded casserole dish over a high heat. Season the pork cheeks with sea salt then sear on all sides until well coloured. Remove from the dish and set aside.

Place the onion, carrot, garlic, bay leaf, and sweet paprika in the dish and cook, stirring for a few minutes to colour the vegetables a little. Pour in the red wine and bring to a simmer for a few minutes to burn off the alcohol. Add the pork cheeks and chicken stock and bring to a simmer. Cover the pot with a lid and place in the oven for 2 hours 30 minutes to braise.

Meanwhile, prepare the sauce. Heat half the olive oil in a pan over a medium heat and add the bread. Sauté, stirring until golden, then remove from the pan and reserve.

Heat the remaining olive oil in the pan, then add the garlic and cook until golden. Add the onions along with a good sprinkling of salt, then sweat it down while stirring until soft and transclucent. Add the red pepper and continue cooking until softened. Stir in the chopped tomatoes, sweet and hot paprika then turn the heat down and simmer very gently until the mixture becomes jam-like in texture (about 20 minutes). Add the reserved toasted bread to the pan and set aside to finish before serving.

Once the cheeks are cooked carefully drain in a colander, reserving the liquid. Discard the solids. Pour 400 ml (14 fl oz) of the reserved liquid and pour over the sauce base. Bring to a simmer and cook for 5 minutes. Pour into a food processor or blender and pulse until smooth. Pass through a fine sieve and pour back into a pan large enough to hold the cheeks. Season with a little coarse sea salt, add the cheeks and bring back to a simmer to heat through. Serve with creamed potatoes and a simple green salad.

Ribeye steak with wood-roasted peppers and sautéed potatoes

Txuletoia pikillo piper eta patata salteatuekin

Chuletón con pimientos de piquillo y patatas salteadas

The Basque Country produces some of the most amazing grass-fed beef and the people have mastered the art of cooking huge slabs of beef forerib or *chuletón* over coals, producing a thick smoky crust and red juicy interior.

The Basques also take their cider pretty seriously. The official cider season kicks off in mid January and runs for around three months. During this time, locals (and informed tourists) frequent cider houses or *sagardotegis* to eat chuletón washed down with copious amounts of extremely dry apple cider. Traditionally the locals would take their own meat to the *sagardotegis* and the host would cook it in good faith that the punter would buy their cider.

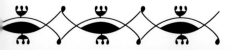

SERVES 4

1.5 kg (3¼ lb) forerib of beef on the bone

Coarse sea salt

60 ml (4 tablespoons) olive oil, plus more for frying

800 g (1¾ lb) baby new potatoes, cut into quarters lengthways

3 garlic cloves, peeled and finely sliced

250 g (9 oz) tinned piquillo peppers in brine, drained

Rub the surface of the meat with salt and olive oil then leave out of the refrigerator for at least 30 minutes to come to room temperature.

Place the potatoes in a pan and cover with cold water. Season with a sprinkling of salt, bring to a simmer and cook until tender but not falling apart. Drain in a colander and set aside until serving.

Preheat the oven to 180°C/350°F/Gas mark 4.

Heat a large heavy frying pan over medium to high heat. Sear the ribeye on both sides until it has a dark crust. Place the beef on a rack in a roasting tray and and roast for approximately 10 minutes for rare, 15 for medium or 30 for well done. Cooking times will vary depending on the thickness of the meat so I recommend using a meat thermometer and inserting it into the centre of the forerib: it will measure 50°C/125°F for rare, 60°C/140°F for medium and 70°C/155°F for well done.

Once the beef is cooked to your liking remove from the oven and cover loosely with aluminium foil. Leave to rest for at least 10 minutes for the fibres to relax and the juices to dissipate through the flesh. Doing this will make the meat juicier and more tender.

Meanwhile, finish off the potatoes and piquillo peppers. Heat 2 tablespoons of olive oil over a low heat. Add the sliced garlic and slowly cook for 2–4 minutes to infuse the oil. As the garlic starts to turn golden add the piquillo peppers, turn the heat down to very low and keep warm while finishing the potatoes.

Heat a film of olive oil in a frying pan over high heat. Add the potatoes and a good sprinkling of salt, and sauté until golden and heated through.

To serve, run a sharp knife along the forerib bone to remove the flesh in a large piece. Slice into 2.5 cm (1 in) thick slices, transfer to a serving platter and sprinkle with a little coarse sea salt. Rest the bone next to the sliced beef as though you are rebuilding the forerib and spoon the piquillo peppers over the top. Serve the sautéed potatoes in a separate dish to pass around the table.

White bean stew with chorizo, morcilla and pancetta

Asturiar fabada

Fabada asturiana

A popular bean dish originating in Spain's northern region of Asturias, *fabada* is so popular that just about every supermarket throughout the country will sell a canned variety. It's actually quite good, but of course it's better to cook your own. Traditionally it's only made with the rare *fabes de la granja* bean, which is difficult to find outside of Spain, but it's perfectly acceptable to use cannellini or butter beans instead. Make sure to soak the beans for at least 12 or even 24 hours if you have the time. Boiling them first helps in their cooking.

White bean stew with chorizo, morcilla and pancetta

SERVES 4

400 g (14 oz) dried white kidney beans or butter (fava) beans
   soaked in cold water for at least 12 hours
250 g (9 oz) morcilla
45 ml (3 tablespoons) olive oil
1 medium onion, peeled and finely diced
1 bay leaf
½ teaspoon sweet paprika
Pinch of saffron threads
5 garlic cloves, peeled
25 g (1 oz) chunk of tocino salado (salted pork back fat)
150 g (5 oz) cooking chorizo
150 g (5 oz) pancetta
1 litre (1¾ pints) white chicken stock (see Basics)
Coarse sea salt

Drain the soaked beans, place into a large pan and cover with cold water. Place over high heat and bring to the boil. Leave to boil vigorously for 10 minutes, remove from the heat and drain in a colander.

Peel the skin off 100 g (3½ oz) of the morcilla, crumble into small pieces and set aside until serving.

Heat 30 ml (2 tablespoons) of the olive oil in a large pan over medium heat. Add the onion and bay leaf and sweat down until soft. Add the paprika, saffron, garlic and *tocino salado* and continue sweating down for another 2 minutes.

Add the chorizo, pancetta, the remaining morcilla and the beans and pour over the chicken stock. Bring to a gentle simmer and cook for about 2 hours or until the beans are soft but not falling apart, making sure the beans are constantly covered with liquid. Check the beans every 15 minutes after an hour of cooking and add a little water if needed.

When the beans are ready, remove the pan from the heat and discard the bay leaf and tocino salado. Scoop out the chorizo, morcilla and pancetta and slice thickly. Stir back through the beans, add a little salt to taste and transfer to a serving dish or divide between four warm bowls.

Heat the remaining olive oil in a frying pan over high heat, add the crumbled morcilla and sauté for about 30 seconds or until crisp. Sprinkle over the fabada just before serving.

Grilled lamb cutlets with red mojo sauce and chopped pepper salad

Arkume txuletak pipirrana eta mojo gorriarekin

Chuletitas de cordero con pipirrana y mojo rojo

Lamb cutlets are delicious and perfect to grill or barbecue, as the layer of fat surrounding the flesh melts during cooking, keeping the meat moist and succulent. *Pipirrana* is simply a salad of chopped vegetables popular in the hotter parts of Spain. Each region has its own versions which sometimes contain bread, tuna and eggs. I've kept my version pretty simple, as the mojo rojo is the main seasoning of the dish. The tangy *mojo rojo* cuts into the slightly fatty lamb perfectly and the finely diced pipirrana adds crunch and freshness.

Grilled lamb cutlets with red mojo sauce and chopped pepper salad

SERVES 4

12 lamb cutlets
1 teaspoon coarse sea salt
2 garlic cloves, peeled and finely sliced
60 ml (4 tablespoons) olive oil

PIPIRRANA

½ small Italian white onion, peeled and cut into a small dice
2 plum tomatoes
½ red bell pepper (capsicum), deseeded, membrane removed and cut into a pea-sized dice
½ green bell pepper (capsicum), deseeded, membrane removed and cut into a pea-sized dice
1 small Lebanese cucumber, cut into a pea-sized dice
1 baby gem lettuce
75 ml (5 tablespoons) extra virgin olive oil
20 ml (4 teaspoons) white wine vinegar
½ garlic clove, peeled and ground to a paste with ½ a teaspoon of salt
Coarse sea salt

TO SERVE

200 ml (7 fl oz) mojo rojo (see Basics)

Place the lamb cutlets in a dish and, using your hands, massage the salt, garlic and olive oil into the meat. Set aside to marinate for 30 minutes.

Meanwhile, prepare the *pipirrana*. Place the diced onion in a bowl, cover with cold water and leave to soak for 10 minutes. Cut the tomatoes into quarters, remove and discard the seeds. Cut the flesh into small dice and put in a mixing bowl with the diced peppers and cucumber. Drain the onion in a sieve. Pat dry with paper towels, then add to the mixing bowl. Cut the base off the baby gem lettuce and discard the large outer leaves. Remove the leaves individually, so you have 12 lettuce leaf cups in total. Wash and pat dry with paper towels.

To finish the dish, heat a grill or barbecue until nearly smoking hot. While the grill is heating dress the pipirrana with the olive oil, white wine vinegar and garlic. Toss together with a sprinkling of sea salt then set aside for the flavours to meld.

Place the lamb on the grill and sear for 3 minutes each side, or longer if you prefer well done. Remove from the grill and leave to rest in a warm place for a few minutes. Place the cutlets on a serving dish. Divide the pipirrana between the baby gem cups and arrange on the platter with the lamb.

Serve the *mojo rojo* on the side or spoon around the lamb.

Oxtail braised in Pedro Ximenez sherry with parsnip purée and pancetta

Zezen-isatsa Pedro Ximenez erara chiribi-purea eta hirugiharrarekin

Rabo de toro al Pedro Ximenez con puré de chirivía y panceta

Rich, sticky and full of flavour, slow-braised oxtail is one of the tastiest beef dishes of all. The combination of red wine and Pedro Ximenez in the braising liquid creates a perfect sauce to be soaked up by the earthy parsnip purée. To finish the dish off, the slightly salty pancetta is the ideal contrast to the sweet parsnip and enforces the meatiness of the oxtail. This dish works really well with other cuts of beef such as the shin or blade steak but beef on the bone such as oxtail delivers the best flavour. Like all braises, this dish tastes better when reheated the next day so if time prevails prepare ahead, then it's just a matter of heating and serving.

Oxtail braised in Pedro Ximenez sherry with parsnip purée and pancetta

Serves 4

1.2 kg (2½ lb) oxtail, separated at the joints
2 tablespoons plain (all-purpose)flour
30 ml (2 tablespoons) olive oil
1 large onion, peeled and cut
   into quarters
1 large carrot, peeled and cut into
   large chunks
2 celery stalks, cut into large chunks
400 ml (14 fl oz) red Rioja wine
600 ml (1¼ pints) Pedro Ximenez sherry
3 garlic cloves, peeled
1 bay leaf
10 peppercorns
4 thyme sprigs
400 ml (14 fl oz) brown chicken stock (see
   Basics)
Coarse sea salt

PARSNIP PURÉE

800 g (1¾ lb) parsnip, peeled and cut into
   small even chunks
2 garlic cloves, peeled
600 ml (1 pint) milk
200 ml (7 fl oz) water
1 bay leaf
Coarse sea salt

TO FINISH

100 g (3½ oz) pancetta, diced
15 ml (1 tablespoon) olive oil

Preheat the oven to 120°C/250°F/Gas mark ½.

Put the oxtail in a bowl and sprinkle the flour over the top. Shake the bowl to coat the oxtail completely, and season with sea salt.

Heat the olive oil in a heavy pan or casserole dish over a high heat and brown the oxtail pieces in batches on all sides. Remove the oxtail from the casserole and set aside.

Place the onion, carrot and celery in the pan and sauté, stirring until golden. Pour in the wine and sherry and bring to a simmer for 5 minutes to burn off the alcohol.

Return the oxtail to the pot along with the garlic, bay leaf, peppercorns and thyme and pour over the stock. Bring to a simmer and skim any froth off the top and discard. Cover with a lid, and put in the oven to braise for 3 hours.

Meanwhile, prepare the parsnip purée. Place the parsnip, bay leaf and garlic in a pan and cover with the milk and water. Bring to a simmer over medium heat and cook until the parsnip crushes easily with the back of a fork. Drain in a colander, reserving the liquid. Place the parsnip into a food processor and pulse to a smooth purée. Add some of the reserved cooking milk if it's a bit dry and season with salt to taste. Set aside until serving and discard any remaining milk.

At the end of the 3 hours the oxtail will fall from the bone so carefully remove each piece from the sauce and set aside. Pass the sauce through a fine sieve and discard the vegetables. Pour the sauce into a pan and place over a medium heat, reduce by half.

To finish, heat a film of olive oil in a frying pan and sauté the pancetta till golden. Place the pancetta onto a paper towel to soak up any excess oil. Return the oxtail to the reduced sauce, season with salt to taste, then place over a low heat to warm through. Meanwhile, reheat the parsnip purée over a low heat. Divide the purée between four plates then put the oxtail on top. Drizzle the sauce around. Scatter over the pancetta.

Roast rump of lamb with roasted aubergine and pepper salad with romesco sauce

Arkume errea eskalibada eta romesko saltsarekin

Cordero asado con escalivada y salsa romesco

This is a really stunning dish full of colour, robust flavours and Catalan flair. It may not be as tender as other cuts; however, lamb rump makes up for it in flavour, as long as you don't overcook it. It's best cooked to medium. Most importantly let the lamb rest in a warm place for about 5 minutes for the meat fibres to relax and for the juices to flow back to the outer edges of the meat.

Escalivada is a traditional Catalan dish of vegetables such as aubergine and pepper, roasted over coals, which imparts a smoky flavour. You can achieve a similar effect using a hot oven. Romesco sauce works fantastically with roasted vegetables and meats and brings this dish together as a whole.

Roast rump of lamb with roasted aubergine and pepper salad with romesco sauce

SERVES 4

> *30 ml (2 tablespoons) aceite de ajo y perejil (see Basics)*
> *4 x 200 g (7 oz) boneless rumps of lamb (chumps)*
> *2 red bell peppers (capsicum)*
> *2 aubergines (eggplants)*
> *2 small onions*
> *1 garlic bulb*
> *45 ml (3 tablespoons) olive oil, plus extra for frying*
> *250 ml (8 ½ fl oz) romesco sauce, (see Basics)*
> *Coarse sea salt*

Preheat your oven to 200°C/400°F/Gas mark 6.

Rub the aceite de ajo y perejil into the lamb rumps and leave to marinate while you prepare the escalivada.

Place the peppers, aubergines, onions and garlic bulb in a roasting tray and drizzle over half the olive oil. Roast in the oven for 20 minutes. Remove the garlic from the tray and set aside to cool. Turn the vegetables over and return to the oven for another 15–20 minutes or until the red pepper skin is blackened and blistered. Remove from the oven and place the red pepper in a small bowl. Cover tightly with cling film (plastic wrap) and set aside until cool enough to handle.

Peel the skin from the vegetables and squeeze the soft garlic from its skin and mash with the back of a fork. Tear the aubergine into strips and place in a large bowl. Tear the peppers into strips, discarding the seeds and place in the bowl with the aubergine. Cut the onions into wedges then add to the other vegetables along with a sprinkling of sea salt and the mashed garlic. Pour the remaining olive oil over the vegetables and toss to combine. Leave at room temperature for the flavours to meld while cooking the lamb.

Heat a film of olive oil in a frying pan over a medium heat. Season the lamb rumps with sea salt and add to the pan, skin side down and sear for about 5 minutes to render some fat out of the skin. Once the skin is gold and crisp sear the other side of the lamb and place on a rack sitting in a roasting tray. Roast in the oven for 8–10 minutes for pink lamb, or longer if you like it more well done. Remove the lamb from the oven, cover with aluminium foil and leave to rest for 5 minutes. At this stage you can warm up the escalivada by placing in a roasting tray and returning it to the oven for 5 minutes.

Arrange the escalivada in rows on a serving platter or divide between four warm plates. Slice the lamb into 1 cm (½ in) thick slices and arrange next to the escalivada. Spoon the romesco sauce over the vegetables or serve on the side.

Ribeye of beef with potato and jamón gratin, girolles and onion and Idiazabal cheese purée

Txuletoia urdaiazpiko eta patata gainerrea, zizak eta Idiazabal purearekin

Chuletón con gratinado de patata y jamón, níscalos y puré de Idiazabal

Spanish jamón is delicious sliced straight from the bone and is also a great ingredient for cooking since its subtle flavour and saltiness seasons whatever it's added to. In this dish jamón serrano is finely chopped then added to a simple potato gratin enriching it and imparting it with an almost smoky flavour. I served a dish similar to this to Michel Roux Jnr during my time on Professional MasterChef UK, and it got me through to the semi finals. *Idiazabal* is a firm-textured smoky-flavoured cheese from the Basque Country made from the milk of the Latxa sheep of the region. Idiazabal is available in good Spanish delicatessens or can be substituted with another firm cheese such as pecorino.

Ribeye of beef with potato and jamón gratin, girolles and onion and Idiazabal cheese purée

SERVES 4

Butter, for greasing

30 ml (2 tablespoons) olive oil

1 small onion, peeled and
    finely sliced

50 g (1¾ oz) jamón serrano, sliced into
    small pieces

1 clove garlic, peeled and minced

800 g (1¾ lb) floury potatoes, peeled

400 ml (14 fl oz) chicken stock

Coarse sea salt

ONION PURÉE

30 ml (2 tablespoons) olive oil

2 medium white Italian onions,
    roughly chopped

1 bay leaf

3 sprigs of thyme

40 g (1½ oz) Idiazabal cheese,
    finely grated

TO SERVE

4 x 200 g (7 oz) ribeye steaks

Coarse sea salt

10 ml (2 teaspoons) aciete de ajo y perejil
    (see Basics)

150 g (5 oz) girolle mushrooms
    (or mushrooms of you choice)

30ml (1 fl oz) Oloroso sherry

Olive oil, for frying

Preheat the oven to 190°C/375°F/Gas mark 5. Generously grease a 20 x 20 x 5 cm (8 x 8 x 2 in) ceramic dish with butter and set aside.

Heat the olive oil in a large pan over medium heat, add the onions, jamón serrano and garlic. Gently sweat down until soft, without colouring. Use a mandolin or sharp knife to finely slice the potatoes and add to the onions and jamón serrano mixture. Pour over the stock, place back on the heat and gently cook, stirring until the potatoes are about half cooked. They should be soft but still hold their shape. Season with salt. Pour the potato mixture in the greased dish. Press down to make a flat layer on the top. Bake for 35–40 minutes. Insert a small knife into the centre to make sure that the potato is completely cooked.

Meanwhile, prepare the onion purée. Heat the olive oil in a small pan over a low heat, and add the onion, bay leaf and thyme. Gently sweat the onion, for a few minutes stirring, making sure not to colour it at all. Reduce the heat to very low. Cover the onion with a disc of baking paper and leave to cook gently for 30 minutes, stirring from time to time so it doesn't stick to the base of the pan. If it looks as if it's getting a little dry add a splash of water.

Remove the thyme sprigs and bay leaf from the onion and discard. Transfer to a food processor along with the grated Idiazabal cheese and purée until smooth. Season with salt to taste, return to the pan and keep warm while finishing the dish.

Season the ribeye steaks on both sides with salt rub and a little olive oil. Heat a heavy frying pan over high heat, add the steaks and cook for 2 minutes. Turn and cook for another 2 minutes or longer if you like them less rare. Remove the steaks from the pan and set aside in a warm place to rest for a few minutes.

Place the pan back over a medium heat and add the *aceite de ajo y perejil*, mushrooms and a sprinkling of salt. Sauté while stirring for 30 seconds then add the sherry to the pan and simmer until reduced to a glaze. Divide the onion purée and mushrooms between four warm plates or sauce pots. Slice each steak on an angle into five pieces then arrange neatly on the plates.

Serve with the gratin in the middle of the table for everyone to help themselves.

Slow-roast lamb shoulder with anchovy, rosemary-crushed butter beans and braised shallots

Arkume errea antxoa, erromero-babarrun eta jerez-ozpin txalotekin

Cordero asado con anchoas, alubias pochadas al romero y chalotas al vinagre de jerez

I've been preparing this dish in one form or another throughout my career. Slow roasting the lamb with a touch of stock results in meat that melts in the mouth, while a quick reduction of the juices creates an amazing sauce to pour over the top. Rubbing chopped anchovies into the skin acts as a seasoning adding a lovely 'umami' flavour. I serve this lamb with a purée of some kind to soak up the lovely juices, and here crushed butter beans add a truly Mediterranean flavour. Sherry vinegar gives a touch of acidity to cut into the fattiness of the lamb, while the shallots deliver sweetness which is the perfect match to the salty anchovy. When you cover the lamb make an airtight seal or it could dry out, so check during cooking and add a touch of water if needed.

Slow-roast lamb shoulder with anchovy, rosemary-crushed butter beans and braised shallots

SERVES 4

7 sprigs of rosemary
125 ml (4 fl oz) extra virgin olive oil
4 garlic cloves, peeled
500 g (1¼ lb) small round golden shallots
50 g (1¾ oz) sugar
100 ml (3½ fl oz) sherry vinegar
500 ml (1 pint) brown chicken stock (see Basics)
1.2 kg (2 ¾ lb) boneless shoulder of lamb
Coarse sea salt
6 salted anchovy fillets in oil, drained and finely chopped
30 g (1 oz) salted butter
200 g (7 oz) dry butter (fava) beans, cooked (see sauces and Basics) or
  2 x 400 g (14 oz) cans of cooked butter beans, drained and rinsed

To make the rosemary oil, strip the leaves from 2 sprigs of rosemary and put in a blender with the olive oil and a clove of garlic. Pulse a few times to roughly chop, pour into a bowl and set aside at room temperature to steep.

Preheat the oven to 120°C/250°F/Gas mark ½.

Peel the shallots making sure to leave the root end attached so they don't fall apart during cooking. Heat a film of olive oil in a frying pan over high heat, add the shallots and sauté until golden all over. Add the sugar and sherry vinegar to the pan and cook until the vinegar has reduced and the shallots are covered with a shiny glaze. Pour into a deep baking dish add the remaining garlic cloves and rosemary and pour over the stock.

In a clean frying pan heat a glug of olive oil. Season the lamb all over with salt and sear on all sides until well coloured. Place the lamb on top of the shallots skin side up and spread the chopped anchovy over the skin.

Use a large piece of aluminium foil to wrap the tray, making sure the foil doesn't touch the lamb. Scrunch the foil around the edges of the tray tightly so none of the liquid evaporates during cooking. Bake for 4 hours 30 minutes. Fifteen minutes before the end of cooking, remove the foil and cook the lamb, uncovered, for another 15 minutes.

Meanwhile in a pan, melt the butter. Add the beans, 200 ml (7 fl oz) of water and a good sprinkling of salt and, using a potato masher, smash up the beans and place in a serving dish. Pass the rosemary oil through a fine sieve discarding the solids and pour over the butter beans.

Remove the lamb from the oven and using a plate as a scoop, transfer to a serving dish. Remove the shallots and place around the lamb, skimming any fat off the liquid remaining in the baking tray. Place the tray over a high heat and bring to boil and reduce till thickened slightly before pouring over the lamb.

Serve in the centre of the table with a simple green salad of baby gem lettuce for everyone to help themselves to.

SWEETS

Gozokiak

DULCES

THE SPANISH OFTEN OVERLOOK DESSERTS AS PART OF A MEAL, and often a fresh piece of fruit or a simple cake will suffice. I prefer to dive a little deeper. The Spanish make the most of skilfully spiced sweets such as the citrusy *crema Catalana* or the cinnamon-scented custards of the Basque Country.

Pastries and cakes are commonly enjoyed at breakfast or for *merienda*, Spain's version of afternoon tea served alongside milky coffee for an afternoon pick-me-up. After dinner, small crunchy pastries such as the custard-filled *milojas* accompany espresso or the milk-stained *cortado*, where espresso is 'cut' with a dash of milk.

I love to take classic Spanish desserts and re-work them into modern dishes, using traditional elements and flavours such as in my *leche frita con plátano or* crema Catalana ice cream with chocolate panna cotta and almond crumbs. These may not be true to the classics but I do try to keep the integrity of the original dish and if it tastes great, why not?

Membrillo and walnut baklava

Irasagar eta intxaur baklava

Baklava de membrillo y nueces

Ever since I was a kid I've loved baklava and was lucky enough to grow up next door to a Cypriot lady who made it almost daily and happily shared it with her neighbours. I still remember licking the rich honey-flavoured syrup from my fingers and yearning for more even though I knew I would have to wait at least until tomorrow for another helping. These days though, I'm lucky enough to be able to make my own and it's the ideal chance to combine the perfect match of walnuts and quince. Baklava definitely isn't a Spanish dessert but I did get the inspiration for this version while eating a cheese plate containing quince paste after a meal in Barcelona. Quince paste or *membrillo* is usually served with cheese, particularly manchego or Idiazabal and it also finds it way into desserts or even spread on toast for breakfast. It's also delicious on its own as a sweet.

Membrillo and walnut baklava

MAKES 32 PIECES

200 g (7 oz) walnuts, coarsely chopped
30 g (1 oz) sugar
½ teaspoon ground cinnamon
300 g (10 oz) pack filo pastry
100 g (3½ oz) unsalted butter

SYRUP
80 ml (2¾ fl oz) water
80 g (3 oz) caster (superfine) sugar
100 ml (3½ fl oz) membrillo (quince paste), roughly chopped
50 ml (1¾ oz) honey

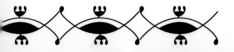

Preheat the oven to 180°C/350°F/Gas mark 4.

Melt the butter and grease a 20 x 20 x 5 cm (8 x 8 x 2 in) baking tray. Line the bottom with a piece of baking paper and set aside. Combine the chopped walnuts, sugar and cinnamon and set aside. Cut the filo sheets the same size as the base of the tray making sure to reserve any trimmings to use in some layers.

Brush the layer of baking paper with butter and press down a layer of filo. Repeat the layering, making sure to butter between each until you have eight layers. Sprinkle over half of the chopped nut mix and repeat the layering process with the pastry to make another eight layers. Use the trimmings for these layers as they don't need to be too neat.

Sprinkle over the remaining nuts and repeat the pastry layering process again until all the filo is used up. You should have about another eight layers on top. Finish by brushing the top layer with butter and put into the refrigerator for 10 minutes for the butter to set.

Before baking, use a knife to cut the baklava into 2.5 x 5 cm (1 x 2 in) rectangles, making sure to cut through all the layers of pastry. Place in the oven and bake for 45 minutes until the top is golden and crisp.

Meanwhile, prepare the syrup. In a small pan combine the water, sugar, *membrillo* and honey. Heat over a medium heat while whisking until the sugar and membrillo have fully dissolved. Pass through a fine sieve and keep hot. Once the baklava is cooked pour the hot syrup along each dividing cut in the baklava and leave to cool. Use a palette knife to remove the individual portions from the tray. Store in an airtight container in a cool place for up to 3 days.

Basque cream with almond tuilles

Natilak teilekin

Natillas con tejas

Smooth creamy custard contrasted with the lightest and crispiest almond biscuits makes *natillas con tejas* the perfect way to end a meal. One of Spain's most traditional desserts, natillas is on just about every family-run restaurant menu, made to a family recipe most likely handed down through the generations. It's a cross between crème anglaise and crème patissière. Natillas takes literally minutes to make and unlike crème anglaise, it won't separate and turn into scrambled eggs if it comes to the boil because the addition of cornflour stabilises it.

It's common to see natillas served with plain packet biscuits, but I like to serve mine with *tejas de Tolosa*, a type of almond tuille common to the town of Tolosa in the Basque region of Spain. Both the natillas and tejas are extremely easy to make and can be made ahead making the duo a perfect dessert for a casual dinner.

Basque cream with almond tuilles

SERVES 4

50 g (1¾ oz) ground almonds
30 g (1 oz) flaked almonds
15 g (½ oz) plain (all-purpose) flour
50 g (1¾ oz) icing (confectioners') sugar
1 egg white
15 g (½ oz) butter

NATILLAS
½ vanilla pod
550 ml (17 fl oz) milk
1 cinnamon stick about 5 cm (2 in) in length
6 egg yolks
85 g (3 oz) caster (superfine) sugar
2 tablespoons cornflour (cornstarch)
Ground cinnamon, for sprinkling

To make the biscuits, in a small mixing bowl, combine the ground almonds, flaked almonds, flour and icing sugar.

In a separate bowl whisk the egg white to soft peaks and fold into the dry mix until well combined. Melt the butter in a small pan over a low heat, add to the mix and stir until thoroughly incorporated. Transfer to a small bowl, cover with cling film (plastic wrap) and refrigerate for at least an hour.

Preheat the oven to 160°C/325°F/Gas mark 3.

Spoon 16 large tablespoons of the mixture onto a baking-paper-lined tray, leaving a large space between each. Cover with a layer of cling film (plastic wrap) and use a flat object or a rolling pin to flatten them into 10 cm (4 in) discs. Peel off the cling film and discard. Bake in batches for 10 minutes or until golden brown. When cooked, use a palette knife to remove them from the tray and, one at a time, drape over a rolling pin to cool, to give them a nice curved shape. When cold, the biscuits will have crisped up. Transfer to an airtight container.

To make the natillas, split the vanilla pod lengthways and scrape out the seeds. Place the seeds and pod in a pan with the milk and cinnamon stick and bring to a simmer. Remove from the heat and set aside. In a bowl, whisk the egg yolks with the sugar and cornflour until pale. While still whisking, slowly pour in the milk mixture, then pour the egg mixture back into the pan and place over a low heat. Continuously stir the mixture with a rubber spatula as it heats and thickens. Once the custard starts to bubble cook for 1 more minute, remove from the heat. Pass the custard through a fine sieve and transfer to a bowl. Press a layer of cling film onto the surface to stop a skin forming and leave to go cold. Refrigerate until ready to serve.

To serve pour the natillas into four serving dishes or glasses and sprinkle with a small amount of ground cinnamon. Serve with the biscuits on the side for dipping.

Chocolate panna cotta with crema catalana ice cream and almond crumbs

Txokolate pannacotta katalan krema izozkia eta almendra kurruskariekin

Panacota de chocolate con helado de crema catalana y crujiente de almendras

This is another recipe I prepared during my appearance on Professional MasterChef and I'm more than happy to share it. The rich chocolate panna cotta is divine, and with the *crema catalana* ice cream it's truly out of this world. Crunchy almond crumbs scented with cinnamon add an interesting contrast in texture and bring the dish together perfectly. It's a rich dessert so I wouldn't recommend serving it in huge portions but, of course, you might not be able to help yourself.

Chocolate panna cotta with crema Catalana ice cream and almond crumbs

SERVES 4

1½ gelatine leaves
¼ vanilla pod
50 g (1 ¾ oz) caster (superfine) sugar
120 ml (4 fl oz) milk
150 ml (5 fl oz) double (heavy) cream
70 g (2½ oz) dark (bittersweet) chocolate, at least 60 per cent cocoa solids

ALMOND CRUMBS

25 g (1 oz) flaked almonds
30 g (1 oz) unsalted butter
45 g (1½ oz) plain (all-purpose) flour
25 g (1 oz) caster (superfine) sugar
½ teaspoon ground cinnamon

TO SERVE

Crema Catalana ice cream (Page 386)

To make the chocolate panna cotta, place the gelatine in a bowl of cold water to soak. Split the vanilla pod and place in a small pan with the sugar, milk and cream over a low heat and bring to a low simmer. Whisk in the chocolate until melted. Drain the gelatine, squeeze out any excess liquid and whisk into the chocolate mixture. Pass the mixture through a fine sieve and leave at room temperature to cool.

Divide the mixture between 4 x 100 ml (3½ fl oz) capacity dariol moulds and refrigerate until set.

Preheat the oven 180°C/350°F/Gas mark 4.

To make the almond crumbs, roughly chop the almonds and place in a mixing bowl with the butter, flour, sugar and cinnamon. Work the mixture with your fingertips until it just comes together but remains quite crumbly. Spread the mixture out on a parchment-lined baking tray and bake for 8 minutes or until slightly golden. Remove from the oven and leave to cool. Break the mix up into smaller crumbly pieces. Store in an airtight container until ready to serve.

To serve, arrange the serving dishes and fill a deep bowl with boiling water. To release the panna cottas from the moulds dip the moulds up to the level of the panna cotta into the water for 2 or 3 seconds. Carefully turn the panna cottas out onto the serving dishes. If it they don't come out easily, dip back into the water for another second or two. Make a small mound of cinnamon crumbs on each plate and place a scoop of crema catalana ice cream on top.

Fried milk custard with caramelised bananas

Peilak banana karamelatuarekin

Leche frita con plátano caramelizado

Leche frita or fried milk is such a classic Spanish dessert that I just had to include it. More of a fried custard, *leche frita* is popular not just in Spain but also throughout Latin countries worldwide. Lightly spiced with cinnamon and orange, the flavour is light and refreshing with a lovely soft texture. Once the custard is prepared it needs a couple of hours to set and it's just a matter of cutting it into fingers and frying it in a little olive oil to create a thin golden crust. *Leche frita* is usually served by itself with a sprinkling of cinnamon, but here I serve it with beautiful caramelised bananas.

Fried milk custard with caramelised bananas

SERVES 4

500 ml (17 fl oz) full-cream milk
5 cm (2½ in) length of cinnamon stick
Zest from ¼ of an orange
1 egg
80 g (3 oz) caster (superfine) sugar
3 tablespoons plain (all-purpose) flour
4 tablespoons cornflour (cornstarch)
20 g (¾ oz) butter

CARAMELISED BANANAS
4 bananas, peeled and each sliced into 3
80 ml (2¾ oz) water
80 g (3 oz) caster (superfine) sugar
30 g (1 oz) butter
5 ml (1 teaspoon) vanilla extract

TO FINISH
3 eggs, whisked until smooth
250 g (9 oz) plain (all-purpose) flour
45 ml (3 tablespoons) vegetable oil
  for frying
Ground cinnamon, for sprinkling
  (optional)

Lightly grease a 20 x 20 cm (8 x 8 in) deep baking tray and line it with a layer of cling film (plastic wrap) (the cling film will stick to the oil). Put the milk, cinnamon and orange zest in a small pan and bring to a simmer. Remove from the heat and leave to steep for 5 minutes.

Meanwhile, in a mixing bowl, whisk the egg and sugar together until creamy. Add the flours and whisk to a smooth paste.

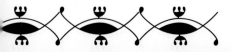

Pass the milk through a fine sieve and discard the solids. While whisking the egg mixture, slowly pour in the milk until well combined. Pour the mixture back into a clean pan and place over a low heat. Continuously stir the mixture with a rubber spatula, making sure to scrape the base of the pan as it heats. When the mixture starts to bubble and is really thick reduce the heat to low and simmer very gently for 10 minutes, stirring regularly. Remove from the heat and beat in the butter.

Pour the custard into the prepared tray and smooth with a flat spatula. Place a layer of cling film directly on top to stop a skin forming and refrigerate for at least 3 hours to set.

To serve, place the flour on a tray and the beaten egg in a bowl. Carefully turn the *leche frita* out onto a chopping board and cut into 12 fingers. Put the fingers in the flour and gently toss to coat. Shake off any excess then toss the fingers in the egg to coat. Place in a colander to drain and set aside.

Heat the oil in a non-stick frying pan over medium-high heat. Now, working in batches, put the leche frita back in the flour and toss to coat. Shake off any excess and put in the hot oil and fry on both sides for a 1–2 minutes or until golden. Remove from pan and transfer to paper towels to soak up the excess oil. Set aside on a plate to cool a little and dust with a small amount of ground cinnamon.

To prepare the bananas, pour half the water into a frying pan and add the sugar. Heat over high heat until the sugar starts to caramelise, add the butter and banana slices. Toss for a few minutes to coat and heat through and add the remaining water and vanilla extract. Continue to shake the pan over the heat for another 30 seconds until the sauce comes together, and remove from the heat.

Divide the fingers between four plates and place a slice of banana on top of each. Pour over any excess caramel from the pan and serve hot.

Basque tart

Euskal pastiza

Pastel vasco

Pastel vasco is a traditional pastry made up of a dense cake crust encasing a soft creamy interior of crème patissière and sometimes, cherries. Every patisserie has their own recipe and during my visits to the Basque Country I've been lucky enough to try dozens of variations of this dessert. Some I've had are almost crunchy on the outside and in this recipe I have re-created this same crunchy shell which contrasts perfectly with the soft creamy interior. They do take a bit of work and they really need to be eaten within a day of making for the best result.

Basque tart

MAKES 4

2 egg yolks
30 g (1 oz) caster (superfine) sugar
1 tablespoon plain (all-purpose) flour
250 ml (8½ fl oz) milk
1 tablespoon cornflour (cornstarch)

CRUST

100 g (3½ oz) unsalted butter, softened
100 g (3½ oz) caster (superfine) sugar
1 egg
Finely grated zest from ½ a lemon
120 g (4½ oz) plain (all-purpose) flour
40 g (4½ oz) self-raising (self-rising) flour
1 egg yolk, beaten, for glazing

To make the custard filling, in a mixing bowl whisk the egg yolks with the sugar until creamy. Add the plain flour and cornflour and whisk thoroughly.

Pour the milk into a pan and bring to a simmer. Pour the hot milk into the bowl with the yolks and sugar while whisking continuously. Pour back into the pan, place over medium heat and bring back to a simmer while whisking. Simmer for another 2 minutes, remove from the heat and pour into a small tray or bowl. Cover with cling film (plastic wrap) directly onto the surface of the custard to stop a skin forming and refrigerate until cold.

To make the crust dough, cream the butter with the sugar until smooth. Beat in the egg and lemon zest until well incorporated. Sieve the flours together and fold into the wet mix to make a soft sticky dough. Wrap with cling film and refrigerate for 30 minutes. Lightly grease four 10 x 2.5 cm (4 x 1 in) deep mini pie tins and place a disc of baking paper in the bottom of each tin.

Preheat the oven to 200°C/400°F/Gas mark 6.

Unwrap the dough and divide into four pieces. Take one piece and cut off about a quarter and set aside. Squash the remaining large piece into one of the tins, using your fingers to line the inside of the pie tin. Make sure to press it into the bottom edge and work it up the edges to form an even layer. Put a quarter of the custard into the lined pastry case and smooth the top with a spoon. Don't worry if you don't use all the dough, just make sure there is a good seal around the crème patissière. Flatten out the reserved piece of dough and place on the top. Seal the edge and smooth out with a wet spoon so the top of the dough is flush with the top of the tin. Repeat with the other three tins, and brush the top of each with egg yolk.

Bake for 20 minutes until gold on top and dark brown on the edges. Carefully turn out from the tins and leave on a cake rack to cool before serving.

Warm chocolate pudding with almond milk ice cream and almond-vanilla praline

Txokolate tarta epela almendra praline eta izozkiarekin

Templado de chocolate con praliné y helado de almendra

Warm soft-centred chocolate cake served with cool creamy almond ice cream is a match made in heaven. I love to add contrasting textures to my food and in this case almond and vanilla praline does the job perfectly. For the chocolate pudding use a good dark chocolate, something between 60–70 per cent cocoa solids is the best – any darker and it can be quite bitter. If you don't have access to an ice cream machine serve the pudding with a good shop-bought vanilla ice cream, it will still be great.

Warm chocolate pudding with almond milk ice cream and almond-vanilla praline

SERVES 4

½ vanilla pod
50 ml (1¾ fl oz) water
50 g (1¾ oz) caster (superfine) sugar
50 g (1¾ oz) almonds (skin on)

PUDDING

Unsweetened cocoa, for dusting
120 g (4½ oz) dark (bittersweet) chocolate, at least 60 per cent cocoa solids
100 g (3½ oz) unsalted butter, plus a little extra for greasing
2 eggs plus 2 egg yolks
100 g (3½ oz) caster (superfine) sugar
25 g (1 oz) plain (all-purpose) flour
50 g (1¾ oz) ground almonds
5 ml (1 teaspoon) vanilla extract
Almond milk ice cream, to serve (Page 390)

To make the almond praline split the vanilla pod lengthways and scrape out the seeds, reserving half for this recipe. Use the remaining seeds to infuse a jar of caster sugar and save for another recipe.

Put the water in a small pan and add the sugar. Combine well and place over a medium heat. Bring to a simmer and leave to cook gently, without stirring. Leave to bubble until the sugar starts to turn a light golden colour, add the almonds and remove from the heat.

Stir in the vanilla seeds, pour onto a baking paper-lined tray and leave to cool. Once cold, place another piece of baking paper on top and gently beat with a rolling pin to crush into crumbs. Alternatively, break up the praline in a food processor until it resembles breadcrumbs.

To prepare the puddings, grease 4 x 150 ml (5 fl oz) pudding moulds. Spoon a little cocoa into each and turn to coat the inside. Tip out the excess.

Preheat the oven to 200°C/400°F/Gas mark 6.

Break up the chocolate and place in a glass bowl with the butter. Bring a small pan of water to a simmer and place the bowl over the water to melt the butter and chocolate. Stir to combine, take the bowl off the heat.

In a mixing bowl, whisk the egg, egg yolk and sugar together until smooth and creamy. Sieve the flour over the top and add the ground almond and whisk until smooth. While still whisking, add the melted butter and chocolate mixture until well combined.

Divide the mixture between the four moulds and bake for 9 minutes. When ready, the puddings will have risen but will be liquid inside. Leave to rest for 1 minute before turning out onto serving dishes next to a spoonful of crushed almond praline. Place a scoop of almond ice cream on the praline and serve immediately.

Caramel poached pears with rice pudding

Udare karamelatuak arrozesnearekin

Peras caramelizadas con arroz con leche

Don't be turned off by the thought of rice pudding as this recipe is nothing like the school dinner or tinned variety that so many people have bad memories of. Lightly spiced with cinnamon and citrus, Spanish *arroz con leche* is light, refreshing and not at all stodgy. Eaten all over Spain and the Latin world, it is usually served cold but is great warm especially in the cooler months. The addition of poached pears may not be traditional but it adds a fantastic contrast to the creamy pudding, while the caramel sauce adds a touch of indulgence.

Caramel poached pears with rice pudding

SERVES 4

120 g (4½ oz) Bomba rice
½ vanilla pod
Peel from ¼ of a lemon, white pith removed
1 cinnamon stick about 5 cm (2 in) long
Few good pinches of ground nutmeg
800 ml (1½ pints) full-cream milk
65 g (2¼ oz) caster (superfine) sugar

PEARS
250 g (9 oz) caster (superfine) sugar
500 ml (17 fl oz) hot water
2 pears, peeled and each cut into 8 wedges with core removed

Soak the rice in cold water for 10 minutes. Rinse under cold running water until it runs clear and pour into a colander to drain for 10 minutes.

Split the vanilla pod lengthways, scrape out the seeds and put into a large pan with the pod. Add the lemon peel, cinnamon sticks, nutmeg, milk and sugar and bring to a simmer. Add the rice, stir to combine, then bring back to a gentle simmer and give another stir. Gently simmer the rice stirring every 10 minutes until cooked, about 30–35 minutes. Remove from the heat and allow to cool. Remove the cinnamon stick, lemon peel and vanilla pod and chill in the refrigerator.

Meanwhile, prepare the pears. Put the sugar in a small pan over a medium heat. After a few minutes the sugar will start to melt around the edges. Use a metal spoon to drag the melted sugar into the granules. Leave for a few more minutes until more sugar has melted and gently stir again. Leave for another few minutes until all the sugar has melted and the sugar starts to turn golden. Keep on the heat until the sugar is a dark golden colour. The whole process should take about 10 minutes.

Remove the pan from the heat and leave for 2 minutes to cool a little. Add the hot water, being careful as it might bubble up and splutter. Return the pan to the heat and bring back to a simmer while stirring until all the caramel has dissolved. Add the pear quarters and gently simmer for 10–15 minutes or until softened but not mushy. The amount of cooking required depends on how ripe the pears are, so check by piercing one with a skewer.

Remove the pan from the heat and allow the pears to cool in the liquid. Once the pears are cold, drain the liquid, reserving half to make a caramel sauce. Put the reserved liquid in a small pan over a medium heat and bring to a simmer. Reduce by half or until thick enough to coat the back of a spoon. Leave to cool.

To serve, remove the rice pudding from the refrigerator 30 minutes before serving. Divide the rice between four bowls and arrange four pieces of pear on each before drizzling with the caramel sauce.

Hazelnut turrón and dark chocolate parfait

Txokolate eta hur-turroi parfait

Parfait de chocolate y turrón de avellana

Popular around Christmas time in Spain, *turrón*, a type of almond nougat of Moorish origin, adorns just about every shop and supermarket shelf throughout the country and is loved by old and young alike. Production is huge and each region has their own specialities which usually fit into two distinct types: *turrón blando* (soft) or *turrón duro* (hard). With such a huge range commercially available, turrón is rarely made at home but it's so simple to prepare its almost criminal not to.

Here I've taken the concept of turrón and turned it into a luscious frozen dessert layered with chocolate parfait. Instead of using the more traditional almond as a flavour I've added hazelnuts, which are a classic combination with chocolate. The parfait is made in two stages with freezing required between each so you will have to make it a day ahead of serving.

Hazelnut turrón and dark chocolate parfait

MAKES 1

½ vanilla pod
250 ml (8½ fl oz) full-cream milk
125 g (4½ oz) dark (bittersweet) chocolate (at least 70 per cent cocoa solids)
4 egg yolks
3½ oz (100g) caster (superfine) sugar
150 ml (5 fl oz) double (heavy) cream

HAZELNUT TURRÓN PARFAIT

40 g (1½ oz) hazelnuts
2 egg whites
20 g (¾ oz) honey
40 g (1½ oz) caster (superfine) sugar
150 ml (5 fl oz) double (heavy) cream

To make the chocolate parfait, lightly grease a 10 x 10 x 25 cm (4 x 4 x 10 in) loaf tin and line with a layer of cling film (plastic wrap) making sure to overhang the edges to wrap over the top when filled.

Split the vanilla pod lengthways and scrape out the seeds. Place the seeds and pod in a pan with the milk and bring to a simmer. Add the chocolate and whisk until melted. Remove from the heat and set aside.

Whisk the egg yolks and sugar together until pale and, while still whisking, slowly add the chocolate milk mix.

Pour back into the pan and place over low heat. Continuously stir with a rubber spatula as it heats until it thickens enough to coat the spatula. You can check the temperature with a sugar thermometer; it is ready when it reaches 77°C/170°F.

Pass the custard through a fine sieve and refrigerate until completely cold. Whisk the double cream to soft peaks and gently fold into the cold chocolate mixture. Pour into the prepared mould and freeze for at least 4 hours.

Preheat the oven to 180°C/350°F/Gas mark 4.

To make the hazelnut turrón parfait, spread the hazelnuts on a baking tray and toast for 7–8 minutes or until a light golden colour and set aside to cool. Once cold, tip the nuts into a plastic bag and, using a small pan, gently bash until coarsely crushed. Whisk the egg whites to soft peaks and set aside.

Place the honey and sugar in a small pan and place over a medium heat, gently stir until the sugar has melted. Remove from the heat and while whisking vigorously slowly pour into the whisked egg whites until well combined. (Don't worry if there are a few small lumps of sugar left, this will only make the texture a little more interesting.) You should end up with a smooth glossy mix. Fold in the toasted hazelnuts and leave at room temperature for an hour or so to cool.

Once the meringue mixture is cold, whisk the double cream to soft peaks and gently fold into the meringue mixture. Pour into the prepared mould over the top of the chocolate parfait and smooth the top with a knife. Fold cling film over the top to seal, and freeze for at least 6 hours before serving.

To serve, wet a cloth with hot water and wipe the outside of the mould to release the parfait from the surface. Tip upside down on a board and tap to remove the parfait. Unwrap the parfait and, using a knife heated under hot water cut the parfait into slices and transfer to cold plates. Any remaining parfait can be wrapped in cling film and frozen for up to a few weeks.

Caramelised French toast with apple compote and vanilla ice cream

Ogi torrada karamelatuak sagar konpota eta bainila izozkiarekin

Torrijas con compota de manzana y helado de vainilla

Every time I see *torrijas* on a menu I can't resist ordering it. There is something so comforting about baked egg custard, especially when it's been soaked into buttery brioche and has a crunchy caramelised crust to crunch through. Apple isn't a traditional addition but it adds a freshness to the dessert and also works fantastically with the vanilla ice cream. In Spain torrijas are traditionally eaten around Easter for breakfast but like most people I'm happy to eat them any time.

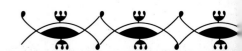

Caramelised French toast with apple compote and vanilla ice cream

SERVES 4

½ square loaf of brioche similar in size to a small loaf of bread
2 eggs
50 g (1¾ oz) caster (superfine) sugar
250 ml (8½ fl oz) milk
250 ml (8½ fl oz) double (heavy) cream

APPLE COMPOTE
1 green apple, peeled and cored
2 tablespoons caster (superfine) sugar
30 ml (2 tablespoons) water
10 ml (2 teaspoons) lemon juice
Zest from ¼ small lemon

TO FINISH
Caster (superfine) sugar, for sprinkling
Vanilla ice cream (See Sweets)

Whisk eggs, sugar, milk and double cream together until smooth, then set aside. Place the brioche in the freezer for 30 minutes to firm it up so it's a bit easier to cut. Using a serrated knife, trim off the crust and cut four rectangles about 4 x 4 x 10 cm (1½ x 1½ x 4 in). Place in a small snug-fitting dish and pour over the egg mixture. Place in the fridge to soak for at least 2 hours.

Meanwhile, prepare the apple compote. Cut the apple into small pea-sized cubes and place in a small pan with the sugar, water, lemon zest and juice. Place over a low heat and gently cook, stirring, until the sugar has dissolved and the apple is soft (about 5–6 minutes, but this can vary depending on the apple so check every couple of minutes). Remove from the heat and leave to cool.

Preheat the oven to 160°C/325°F/Gas mark 3.

Carefully lift the soaking brioche or torrijas from the egg mixture and drain in a colander for 5 minutes. Heat a dry non-stick frying pan over high heat.

Sprinkle the torrijas on each side with a thin covering of sugar and place in the frying pan and sauté for about 1 minute on each side until golden. Transfer to a baking paper-lined baking tray and place in the oven for 5 minutes to warm through. Sprinkle the top of each torrija with about ½ teaspoon caster sugar. Use a gas torch to caramelise the sugar or alternatively place the torrijas on a baking tray under a blazing hot grill to caramelise.

Use a flat spatula to divide the warm torrijas between four plates and spoon a line of apple compote on the side. Place a scoop of ice cream on the compote and serve immediately.

Apple and olive oil cake with walnut streusel and Pedro Ximenez poached sultanas

Sagar tarta intxaur kurruskaria

eta Pedro Ximenez sultana mahaspasekin

Tarta de manzana con crujiente de nueces y

sultanas al Pedro Ximénez

Olive oil is a great substitute for butter in cakes, keeping the texture soft and moist and containing a lot less unhealthy fats. This is a simple cake recipe typically eaten at breakfast time in Spain but I prefer it as a dessert. Here I've made it more of a pudding by adding apple to the mix and serving it with crème anglaise and a bit of a flavour boost from sultanas marinated in sweet Pedro Ximenez sherry. This dessert is best served warm drizzled with cold crème anglaise or a ball of luxury vanilla ice cream.

Apple and olive oil cake with walnut streusel and Pedro Ximenez poached sultanas

SERVES 6

1 egg
75 g (2¾ oz) caster (superfine) sugar
50 ml (1¾ oz) olive oil
50 g (1¾ oz) thick natural
    (plain) yoghurt
160 g (5½ oz) self-raising
    (self-rising) flour
1 granny smith apple, peeled,
    cored and cut into a rough
    pea-sized dice

PEDRO XIMENEZ SULTANAS

120 ml (4 fl oz) Pedro Ximenez
60 g (2 oz) sultanas

STREUSEL TOPPING

30 g (1 oz) walnuts, finely chopped
20 g (¾ oz) unsalted butter, diced
25 g (1 oz) plain (all-purpose) flour
20 g (¾ oz) caster (superfine) sugar
Few pinches ground cinnamon

CRÈME ANGLAISE

½ vanilla pod
125 ml (4¼ fl oz) milk
125 ml (4¼ fl oz) double (heavy) cream
3 egg yolks
30 g (1 oz) caster (superfine) sugar

For the Pedro Ximenez sultanas put the alcohol in a small pan and bring to a simmer over a medium heat. Add the sultanas and continue to cook for 2 minutes, remove from the heat and allow to cool.

Prepare the streusel topping by combining the chopped walnuts, butter, flour, sugar and cinnamon in a mixing bowl. Work the mix with your fingertips until it just comes together.

Preheat the oven to 180°C/350°F/Gas mark 4.

To make the cake, lightly grease six muffin moulds and dust with plain flour. Tap the pan to remove any excess. In a mixing bowl or food processor with a whisk attachment combine the egg and sugar and whisk until smooth. Add the olive oil and yoghurt, whisking until well combined. Sieve the flour into the wet mix and gently fold in until mixed thoroughly. Fold in the diced apple and divide the batter between the six muffin holes. Crumble up the streusel and sprinkle over the top of the cakes making sure to cover the whole surface. Bake for 20 minutes. Test the cakes by inserting a skewer into the centre, it will come out clean when ready.

Meanwhile, prepare the crème anglaise. Split the vanilla pod lengthways and scrape out the seeds. Place the seeds and pod in a pan with the milk and cream and bring to a simmer. Remove from the heat and set aside. Whisk the egg yolks and sugar together until pale and, while still whisking, slowly pour in the milk mixture. Pour back into the pan and place over low heat. Continually stir the mixture with a rubber spatula as it heats until it is thick enough to coat the spatula. It is ready when it reaches 77°C/170°F on a sugar thermometer. Pass the custard through a fine sieve and refrigerate until cold.

To serve make a pool of crème anglaise on each plate. Turn the cakes out and place in the crème anglaise and drizzle the Pedro Ximenex sultanas and syrup.

Caramelised pastry filled with custard cream

Kremazko milorria

Milhojas de crema

Served with coffee, nothing beats *milhojas* for afternoon tea or after a meal. Every bite is a pleasure as your teeth crunch through crispy caramelised pastry to meet a soft creamy filling of vanilla custard. Texturally it's perfect, but it has to be eaten fresh as the pastry starts to soften almost as soon as it's made. The components can be prepared up to a few days beforehand and it takes just a matter of moments to put them together making this the perfect dinner party sweet.

Caramelised pastry filled with custard cream

MAKES 8 SLICES

3 egg yolks
50 g (1¾ oz) caster (superfine) sugar
20 g (¾ oz) 2 tablespoons plain (all-purpose) flour
½ vanilla pod, split lengthways
250 ml (8½ fl oz) milk

PASTRY

2 tablespoons caster (superfine) sugar
30 ml (2 tablespoons) water
150 g (5¼ oz) puff pastry
¾ oz (25g) flaked almonds, toasted until golden
Icing (confectioner's) sugar, for dusting

To make the pastry cream, in a mixing bowl whisk the egg yolks with the sugar until creamy. Add the flour and whisk in thoroughly. Scrape the seeds from the vanilla pod and put both in a pan with the milk. Bring to a simmer, and while whisking, pour into the egg mixture. Pour back into the pan and place over medium heat. Bring to a simmer while whisking and leave to cook for 2 minutes.

Pour into a bowl or tray and top with a piece of buttered baking paper to stop a skin forming. Refrigerate until cold.

To prepare the pastry, combine the sugar and water in a small saucepan and bring to a simmer until the sugar has dissolved.

Preheat the oven to 180°C/ 350°F/Gas mark 4.

Cut the puff pastry into three rectangles and roll each out to 30 x 10 cm (12 x 4 in). Place on a baking tray lined with baking paper and brush each with sugar syrup. Bake for 10 minutes. Remove from the oven and use another tray to press the pastry sheets so they are puffed up no more than 5 mm (¼ in). Carefully turn each over and brush the other side with sugar syrup. Return to the oven and cook for another 10 minutes or until crisp and a dark golden brown. Leave to cool before building the *milhojas*.

Carefully spread half of the pastry cream in an even layer over one piece of pastry. Arrange another piece of pastry on top and spread the remaining pastry cream over. Press the remaining piece of pastry on top and sprinkle over the toasted almonds. Use a serrated knife to cut the milhojas into 2.5 cm (1 in) slices and dust with icing sugar before serving.

Brown butter and almond cakes

Almendra eta gurin-erre mokaduak

Bocado de almendra y mantequilla quemada

The Basques really know how to bake and I was given this recipe by a friend whose Basque mother had passed it onto her. When I tried the original I had to have the recipe – they're so damn good, and I was also surprised at how they're made. Unlike most cake recipes the butter is cooked until it's brown before adding to the mix, which gives the finished cakes a beautiful nutty flavour. It's quite common throughout Spain to eat small cakes and pastries for breakfast but I quite often serve miniature versions of these as a petite four at dinner parties. Whatever time you eat them, make sure they are freshly baked as they dry out quite quickly.

I cook these in small rubber silicone moulds but well-greased mini muffin tins work equally well. To make it a little easier, melt the butter and use a small pastry brush to brush the moulds.

Brown butter and almond cakes

Makes 30

75 g (2 ¾ oz) unsalted butter, plus extra for greasing
½ vanilla bean
50 g (1¾ oz) plain (all-purpose) flour
50 g (1¾ oz) ground almonds
150 g (5 oz) caster (superfine) sugar
4 egg whites
50 g (1¾ oz) flaked almonds

Preheat the oven to 200°C/400°F/Gas mark 6.

Generously grease the mini muffin tins with unsalted butter and set aside.

Melt the butter in a pan over medium heat. Continue cooking the butter while scraping the bottom of the pan until it becomes brown and has a nutty scent. Take off the heat and pour into a ceramic or glass bowl to cool. Don't leave it in the pan as it will continue to cook and burn.

Split the vanilla seed, scrape out the tiny seeds and whisk into the melted butter. You can reserve the vanilla pod casing for another use.

In a mixing bowl, combine the flour, ground almonds and sugar.

In another bowl whisk the egg whites to stiff peaks and gently fold into the dry mixture. Pour in the melted butter and gently stir until well combined.

Put 1 tablespoon of mixture into each prepared mould and sprinkle each individual cake with a few shaved almonds. Bake for 10–12 minutes or until golden. Leave to cool for 5 minutes, turn out of the moulds and leave on a cake rack to cool completely.

Olive oil chocolate pokeys

Palitos de chocolate

Txokolatezko makiltxoak

It might be a little strange to some but a common after-dinner snack in Spain is a piece of dark chocolate eaten with a chunk of bread drizzled with olive oil. The flavours work surprisingly well so I borrowed them to create a version of one of my favourite sweet snacks, the chocolate pokey, more commonly seen in Asian sweet shops. Serve upright in a small glass for a playful sweet with coffee or as an after-dinner petite four. If you want to take it to another level, roll in crushed nuts while the chocolate is still soft.

Olive oil chocolate pokeys

MAKES ABOUT 40

80 g (3 oz) plain (all-purpose) flour
½ teaspoon icing (confectioners') sugar
¼ teaspoon baking powder
30 ml (2 tablespoons) olive oil
30 ml (2 tablespoons) milk
80 g (3 oz) dark (bittersweet) chocolate, 55 per cent cocoa solids

Sieve the flour, icing sugar and baking powder together and place in a food processor. Add the olive oil and pulse the mixture until it resembles breadcrumbs. Add the milk and pulse again for 10 seconds to mix the dough thoroughly. At this stage it still quite crumbly so pour into a mixing bowl and use your hands to squash the dough together. Kneed for 30 seconds and wrap in cling film (plastic wrap) and refrigerate for 30 minutes.

Preheat the oven to 160°C/325°F/Gas mark 3.

Unwrap the pastry and roll out to a thickness of 3 mm (¹⁄₈ in) and chill once more for another 20 minutes or until firm. Cut into 10 cm x 3 mm (4 x ¹⁄₈ in) logs and arrange on a tray lined with baking paper. Make sure they aren't touching or they will stick together when cooking. Bake for 15 minutes or until slightly golden and crisp, remove from the oven and leave to cool.

Place the chocolate in a glass bowl sitting over a pan of simmering water until melted, making sure not to get any water in the chocolate or it will turn grainy.

To coat the pokey sticks with chocolate, turn a shallow baking tray over so the underside is facing up. Place a sheet of baking paper on the upturned tray and pour the melted chocolate on top. One by one, roll the pokey sticks in the chocolate covering the top three-quarters with chocolate. Shake off any excess chocolate and arrange on another tray lined with baking paper. Repeat with all the pokey sticks and refrigerate for 20 minutes to set the chocolate. Pack in an airtight container and store in a cool place for up to 2 days.

Crema catalana ice cream

Katalan krema izozkia

Helado de crema catalana

I just love *crema catalana*, with its almost floral flavour from the infusion of citrus and cinnamon. It also works fantastically as an ice cream which goes especially well with chocolate desserts.

MAKES ABOUT 1 LITRE (1¾ PINTS)

1 vanilla pod	*500 ml (1 pint) full-cream milk*
Zest of 1 lemon	*500 ml (1 pint) double (heavy) cream*
Zest of 1 orange	*12 egg yolks*
2 cinnamon sticks, each about 5cm (2 in) long	*200 g (7 oz) caster (superfine) sugar*

Split the vanilla pod lengthways, scrape out the seeds and place both seeds and pod in a pan. Add the lemon zest, orange zest, cinnamon sticks, milk and cream and place over a low heat. As soon as it comes to a simmer remove from the heat and set aside.

In a large mixing bowl, whisk together the egg yolks and caster sugar. While still whisking slowly pour in the infused milk mixture along with the vanilla, lemon, orange and cinnamon. Once thoroughly combined, pour back into the pan and place over low heat. Continuously stir the mixture with a rubber spatula as it heats making sure to scrape the bottom of the pan as it thickens. Once it's thick enough to coat the back of the spatula it's ready, so remove from the heat or it will overcook and split. If you have a thermometer, cook until it reaches 77°C/170°F. Pass the hot custard through a fine sieve, discard the solids and refrigerate until cold.

Pour the cold custard into an ice cream machine and churn until frozen. Transfer to a lidded plastic tub and freeze for at least 3 hours before serving.

Vanilla ice cream

Bainila izozkia

Helado de vainilla

One of my first jobs when I entered a professional kitchen was to prepare the fresh ice creams and sorbets on a daily basis. I remember being so surprised at just how simple the task was and I couldn't believe that I could make something so nice with just a few simple ingredients. For the best results you really do need an ice cream machine, which slowly churns as it freezes. It is still possible to make a decent ice cream without a machine by putting it in the freezer and giving it a good stir every 20 minutes or so as it freezes, but a machine will give smoother results. I use a basic base recipe for all my ice creams, which is simply crème anglaise or a cooked egg custard, but there are a few things to keep in mind when preparing it. I always use free-range eggs and full-cream milk for richness and when cooking the base make sure it doesn't get too hot or the eggs will scramble and you'll have to start again. I recommend using a thermometer to prevent this happening.

MAKES ABOUT 1 LITRE (1¾ PINTS)

1 vanilla pod
500 ml (1 pint) full-cream milk
12 egg yolks
200 g (7 oz) caster (superfine) sugar
500 ml (1 pint) double (heavy) cream

Split the vanilla pod lengthways and scrape out the seeds. Place the seeds and pod in a pan with the milk and cream and bring to a simmer. Remove from the heat and set aside.

Whisk the egg yolks and sugar together until pale and while still whisking slowly pour in the hot vanilla-infused milk.

Pour back into the pan and place over low heat. Continuously stir the mixture with a rubber spatula as it heats until it thickens enough to coat the spatula. You can check the temperature with a sugar thermometer, it is ready when it reaches 77°C/170°F.

Pass the custard through a fine sieve and refrigerate until completely cold. Pour into an ice cream machine and churn until frozen. Transfer to a lidded plastic tub and freeze for at least 3 hours before serving.

Almond milk ice cream

Almendra-esne izozkia

Helado de leche de almendra

I love the subtle flavour of almonds and their natural creaminess makes them perfect for making ice cream. I've played around with this recipe over the years using different types of almonds and toasting them to different degrees, which changes the flavour significantly. For the best result, a light toasting boosts the flavour of the almonds while not giving a flavour that can be overwhelming. Almond ice cream goes well with just about anything but I think its best served with a chocolate dessert or with warm poached stone fruits.

MAKES ABOUT 1 LITRE (1¾ PINTS)

200 g (7 oz) flaked almonds
600 ml (1¼ pints) full-cream milk
600 ml (1¼ pints) double (heavy) cream
12 egg yolks
200 g (7 oz) caster (superfine) sugar

Preheat the oven to 180°C/350°F/Gas mark 4.

Spread the flaked almonds on a baking tray and toast for 7–8 minutes or until lightly golden and place into a pan with the milk and cream. Bring to a simmer over medium heat, remove from the heat and leave to steep for an hour.

In a mixing bowl, whisk the egg yolks and sugar together until pale. While still whisking, slowly pour in the milk and almond mixture.

Pour the mixture back into the pan and place over low heat. Continuously stir the mixture with a rubber spatula as it heats until it thickens enough to coat the spatula. You can check the correct temperature with a sugar thermometer; it's ready when it reaches 77°C/170°F.

Pass the custard through a fine sieve, discard the almonds and refrigerate until cold.

Once cold, pour into an ice cream machine and churn until frozen. Transfer to a lidded plastic tub and freeze for at least 3 hours before serving.

INDEX

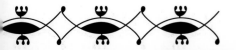

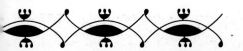

UK: £19.99